Judo & American Culture

Prelude, Acceptance, Embodiment

An Anthology of Articles from the *Journal of Asian Martial Arts*
Edited by Michael A. DeMarco, M.A.

Disclaimer
Please note that the authors and publisher of this book are not responsible in any manner whatsoever for any injury that may result from practicing the techniques and/or following the instructions given within. Since the physical activities described herein may be too strenuous in nature for some readers to engage in safely, it is essential that a physician be consulted prior to training.

All Rights Reserved
No part of this publication, including illustrations, may be reproduced or utilized in any form or by any means, electronic or mechanical, including photocopying, recording, or by any information storage and retrieval system (beyond that copying permitted by sections 107 and 108 of the US Copyright Law and except by reviewers for the public press), without written permission from Via Media Publishing Company.

Warning: Any unauthorized act in relation to a copyright work may result in both a civil claim for damages and criminal prosecution.

Copyright © 2015 by
Via Media Publishing Company
941 Calle Mejia #822
Santa Fe, NM 87501 USA
E-mail: md@goviamedia.com

All articles in this anthology were originally published in the *Journal of Asian Martial Arts*.
Listed according to the table of contents for this anthology:

Wingard, G. (2009)	Volume 18 Number 1	pages 8–21
Hlinak, M. (2009)	Volume 18 Number 2	pages 8–19
Svinth, J. (1999)	Volume 8 Number 1	pages 30–43
Svinth, J. (1998)	Volume 7 Number 1	pages 28–47
Webb, J. (2003)	Volume 12 Number 2	pages 64–73
Behrendt J. (2001)	Volume 10 Number 4	pages 88–91

Book and cover design by Via Media Publishing Company

Edited by Michael A. DeMarco, M.A.

Cover illustration
Painting by Curtis Parker. • www.curtisparker.com

ISBN: 978-1-893765-15-3

www.viamediapublishing.com

contents

iv **Preface**
Michael DeMarco, M.A.

v **Author Bio Notes**

CHAPTERS

1 Building Men on the Mat:
Traditional Manly Arts and the Asian Martial Arts in America
by Geoffrey Wingard, M.Ed.

17 Judo Comes to California:
Judo vs. Wrestling in the American West, 1900–1920
by Matt Hlinak, M.A., J.D.

33 Masato Tamura, Ryoichi Iwakiri, and the Fife Judo Dojo, 1923–1942
by Joseph R. Svinth, M.A.

49 The School of Hard Knocks:
Seattles Kurosaka / Tentoku Kan Dojo 1928–1942
by Joseph R. Svinth, M.A.

69 American Judo Pioneer Vince Tamura and Heike-ryu Jujutsu
by James Webb, M.A.

80 Judo and Character: Moving from the Hard to the Gentle Way
by James Behrendt

85 **Index**

preface

The origins of Asian martial arts in the United States reach back to the Pacific Rim and immigration. This anthology is dedicated to the profoundly significant period—roughly from mid-eighteenth century to the mid-nineteenth century—in which gifted Japanese taught their brand of jujutsu/judo to small groups that gradually disseminated knowledge of combatives into the American mainstream.

In the the first chapter, Geoffrey Wingard provides insightful coverage of the "manly arts" in America as they swept the land along with moving populations. Of course early historical influences came from European groups and their varities of combatives, such as wrestling, boxing, and fencing. Wingard demonstrates that the martial arts are integral to American society and are not ad hoc additions to contemporary popular culture. This background is a prerequisite for understanding the reception of Asian martial arts into American culture.

Matt Hlinak analyzes Japanese-American immigration into the American West through the prism of athletics, specifically by examining a series of contests between judoka and wrestlers from 1900 to 1920 in California. These matches appealed to an interest in Japanese culture, a desire to see stereotypes reinforced, and nationalist tendencies during an age of uncertainty.

The next two chapters by Joseph Svinth detail the establishment and functioning of two important dojos in the Seattle, Washington, area. In 1923 farmers donated a barn and arranged for Ryoichi Iwakiri (third dan) to teach judo to community youths. Another dojo opened in 1928 under the tutalage of Kurosaka Hiroshi (third dan judo). A colorful history marks these dojos and their practitioners: exhibitions, intraclub tournaments, and war-time influences on practice. Their members helped spread judo throughout the United States.

James Webb's chapter focuses on one of the early prime movers for the growth and establishment of judo in America: Vincent Tamura. He was chosen to represent the United States at the First World Championship of Judo (Tokyo, 1956). He is a descendent of the Taira clan, influential during the end of the Heian period (784–1184) in Japan, and his practice has roots in ancient Heike-ryu jujutsu.

Putting academic detail aside, James Behrendt offers a personal account of his early years as a judoka devoted to hard training and competition. He writes "I was extremely fit and strong and I used those natural gifts to eventually defeat the purpose of the judo art. I had discipline but was lacking in spirituality and character." Polishing judo skills helped build his character in the fashion that Kodokan judo founder Kano Jigaro intended.

In these chapters you will find the early hotbeds of jujutsu/judo in America and see how these arts tumbled with European-American "manly arts," making their own way across the country to form and strengthen judo centers in various states. The authors have utilized their scholarly and practical experience to present a rare view of judo as it traversed the Pacific to enrich American culture. Their writings should clarify the early history of judo in America and bring both practitioners and armchair scholars a deeper appreciation for the art.

                                    Michael A. DeMarco
                                    Santa Fe, NM
                                    October 2015

author bio notes

James Behrendt began studying judo in 1954, when he was a young marine stationed in Opama, Japan. He studied under Maseo Ichinoe. In the United States Mr. Behrendt studied with John Osako and Mas Tamura in Chicago. His love of competition led to his winning the Iowa State Championships, then the regional finals of the Pan Am Games. For many years he has been teaching judo in San Diego, California, nurturing the application of judo's philosophy to everyday life. Mr. Behrendt's experience includes four years in an Augustinian community, studying psychology and philosophy.

Matt Hlinak, M.A., J.D. is an academic coordinator and lecturer for the School of Continuing Studies at Northwestern University. He is also an adjunct professor at Ellis University. His teaching and research interests include sport and society, communications law, employment law, literature, and communications. He holds a J.D. from the University of Illinois and an M.A. from Northwestern University. In addition, he has more than twelve years of martial experience, including wrestling, jujutsu, and taekwondo. He recently won his division at the NAGA Midwest Submission Grappling Championships.

Joseph R. Svinth, M.A. received a master's degree in history from the University of Washington in 1983. Mr. Svinth teaches Goju-ryu karate in Seattle, Washington. After researching the history of combative sports in the Japanese and Korean communities of the Pacific Northwest before 1950, he eventually published a book on the subject: *Getting a Grip: Judo in the Nikkei Communities of the Pacific Northwest, 1900–1950* (2003, Tunwater, WA: EJMA).

James Webb, M.A., was educated at West Point, graduating in 1976. He has since received master's degrees in engineering and business. He has studied judo and jujutsu since 1966, for the past twenty years under Vince Tamura. The former national judo champion holds sixth-degree rankings in both judo and jujutsu, a second-degree rank in karate, and is currently the treasurer of the U.S. Judo Association.

Geoffrey Wingard, M.Ed. is a secondary-school teacher and a former college instructor and police officer. He holds an M.A. in Asian history and an M.Ed. in social studies education from the University of Maine. He is also a Maine Criminal Justice Academy graduate. Mr. Wingard began his martial arts training in Moo Duk Kwan taekwondo in 1984. Since 1994 he has trained in Shotokan karate. He holds dan ranks in Moo Duk Kwan taekwondo and Shotokan karate and teaches Shotokan in Orono, Maine.

Building Men on the Mat: Traditional "Manly Arts" and the Asian Martial Arts in America

by Geoffrey Wingard, M.Ed.

Painting by Curtis Parker.
www.curtisparker.com

Introduction

In the post-World War II era, the commodification and dissemination of martial sports based upon traditional Asian fighting methodologies has become a prevalent feature of American culture. The institution and popularization of these martial activities at all levels of society—and the prevailing opinion that they are legitimate forms of recreation and physical and moral education for children and adults—is commonly seen as an example of the development of a new institution in American society. This phenomenon is either an outgrowth of cultural globalism or a corollary to America's appropriation of the traditions and cultures of occupied and colonized peoples. However, the adaptation of Asian martial arts into American society is not a break with American tradition, nor is it an example of a recently developed institution in America. Rather, the popularization of martial arts and combative sports based upon anachronistic Asian fighting methodologies should be viewed as the continuation of a long-standing American process of adapting various traditional, often elite, martial methodologies into American popular culture. The American appropriation and dissemination of martial methodologies from a variety of nations at various times and the publicization of diverse forms of violent recreation, self-protection and militaristic character education is a trend that may be observed not only today, but throughout American history.

While the development of practical fighting skills has certainly been important to Americans for a variety of reasons, the expansion of opportunities to practice martial arts in America in the past half-century seems unprecedented. As sociologist Max Skidmore states, "There is hardly a community of any size in Europe and the English-speaking lands in which there is no instruction available in one or more of the martial arts" (Skidmore, 1995: 129).

However, the practice of all sorts of fighting styles, sports, and techniques has a long history in America. Italian and French fencing schools proliferated at times in early American urban areas (Nadi, 1943: 22). Instruction in English fencing, notably instruction in the English small-sword, was extant in North America from the colonial period at least through the end of the 18th century (Blackwell, 1734). Truly American fighting methods developed unique characteristics based upon regional norms and practices throughout much of the 19th century (Gorn, 1985: 18–43). The apparent difference between the traditional practice of the exercises and rituals of the manly arts, including fencing and other militaristic combat skills in the pre-World War II era, and the practice of Asian martial arts in America today seems, upon closer inspection, to be one of trappings, terminology, and mythology rather than one of any significant difference in availability of instruction or technical efficacy.

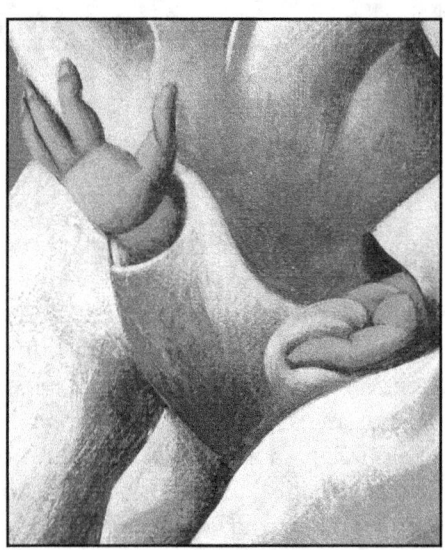

Detail of painting by Curtis Parker.

The difference then is one of appearance rather than substance. The imagery surrounding the martial arts has changed, but their substance and practice in America has not. This imaginary change has occurred for a number of reasons and is not solely, or even primarily, the result of American hegemony in the Pacific following World War II. In fact, the appropriation and Americanization of Asian martial arts began well before Japanese and American military conflict in the Pacific.

It began during the first intensive period of East-West state interaction at the end of the 19th century and early in the 20th century. This was a time when Western public culture, particularly American culture, was engaged in a self-conscious attempt to modernize; yet still relied heavily on traditional institutions. It occurred at a time when the American elite articulated a conscious desire for industrial development and a need to reinforce strong moral and social values in boys and men. At the same time, upper-class social reformers sought to do away with practices and traditions of character education that they felt were embarrassing and anachronistic, so they looked abroad for alternative pedagogical modalities.

One traditional educational venue for the development of courage, strength, and loyalty American boys and men had been through the practice of the manly arts, a compendium of exercises that included games involving the risk of physical trauma or death to foster personal courage and loyalty to the group among participants. However, around the turn of the 20th century, the traditional manly arts, which included practices such as fencing, cudgel fighting, wrestling, and bare-knuckle boxing, had fallen out of public favor and new, modern sports practices had yet to completely fill the void. Modern sports were a new kind of social institution, a complex of behaviors and attitudes that complemented and were completed by industrialism in America while they drew on themes and practices made popular through pre-modern games. In the late 19th and early 20th centuries, amateur and professional sports, as opposed to participatory games, had yet to find universal acceptance.[1] At that time, Western sports proselytizers, Muscular Christians, and physical culture advocates looked abroad for practices they felt could be integrated into the Western masculine milieu and adapted to fill the void left by many elites' (and subsequently the public's) repudiation of the traditional manly arts. They found, developed, and adapted a variety of martial practices from around the world to meet their needs, notably including the new, "scientific" martial art imported from Japan (partially via England) known as judo. Quickly adopted by Victorian dilettantes and Orientalists, judo subsequently became the first of a series of updated and Westernized Asian martial sports to gain widespread popularity in the West.[2]

The study of the appropriation and dissemination of judo in America around the turn of the century reveals a lot about social and cultural developments occurring throughout the country at that time. It has been noted that "how men fight—who participates, who observes, which rules are followed, what is at stake, what tactics are allowed—reveals much about past cultures and societies" (Gorn, 1985: 18). The study of sports in general and the study of physical practices, which, like many martial arts and particularly judo, contain both aspects of traditional masculine contest and modern sport (despite their participants consciously avoiding most types of professional competition), can tell much about the beliefs and ideals of participants and observers. Since modern sport, as defined by sports historian Alan Guttman, can only exist when there is both participation and observation or patronization, the study of modern sports involves the study of people across the social spectrum (Guttman, 1978). The study of sport is not just the study of frequently poor or under-class players, of frequently wealthy patrons, or of working-class and middle-class fans and observers, it is the study of all these groups and, most importantly, it is the analysis of their interactions. Because of the relatively early date of its introduction to the West and because it is a fighting system that was intentionally molded to fit the requirements of a modern sport from its inception, judo is particularly useful to study (Carr, 1993: 169). The study of the introduction and popularization of judo in America can therefore shed light on many issues of concern to social historians, particularly those interested in the complex set of rules and behaviors surrounding violence, social control, and the perpetuation of militaristic education in American society.

The "Manly Arts" in America

Prior to the introduction of judo to the United States at the end of the 19th century, strenuous and frequently violent recreation was subsumed within a category of athletic practices that were popularly known as the "manly arts." The traditional manly arts in America included a variety of public and private practices and games involving the cultivation of strength and spirit. The manly arts as understood by their participants from the late 18th through the early 20th centuries included boxing; wrestling; fencing; stick, staff, and cudgel fighting; gymnastics; and calisthenics, derived from or used to augment military exercises. The manly arts, "the combative arts of the late 1700's through to the early decades of the last century" (Wolf, 2000: 1), were widespread in America as both elites and working-class people sought to strengthen their bodies, compete for prizes and prestige and to emotionally connect with a glorified and virile, although largely mythological, Anglo-Saxon archetype.

Prior to the rise of the professional sports movement in the late 19th and early 20th centuries, there was much less codification of sports and games than exists today and there is a particular dearth of recorded material on the rough and tumble games played by people as recreation from manual, agricultural, and industrial labor. However, these types of pastimes did exist and many people participated in them as sponsors, observers, or players. While the actual number of participants is impossible to determine, the variety of contests and practices and the varied and complex sets of rules and norms applied to combative recreation prior to the advent of the organized sports movement in the late 19th century speaks to the popularity of the manly arts for people of various classes, regions, ethnic, and social backgrounds throughout the United States.

While it may seem absurd to 21st-century observers that the practice of violent forms of recreation would be seen as useful for any purpose other than possible military preparation or popular entertainment, in the 18th and 19th centuries, the cultivation of martial skills were seen as part of the fundamental education of all gentlemen. In America, where an atmosphere of egalitarianism prevailed (at least among a segment of the republican faithful), the idea that there was value in the practice of ritualized violence quickly passed out of elite hands into the public domain. The manly arts and martial recreation became popular, public, and commercial.

This process had already begun by the early 18th century. In 1734, Edward Blackwell, an English immigrant to the American colonies, published a treatise on English fencing with the small sword. In England, small-sword fencing had been the province of gentlemen. The small sword had developed as a weapon for military officers and gentlemen out of the direct line of fire; it was a weapon for personal defense in situations when a saber or firearm would not have been close at hand. In America, however, small-sword fencing was not only the practice of the elite (although elites certainly patronized fencing masters in the 18th century), but quickly became available to the general public. Blackwell published his text on small-sword fencing for the American populace when he found that teaching fencing to the rarified few was neither an acceptable nor very lucrative career in the Colonies. As Blackwell states,

> Having, in my small practice in sundry parts of America, met with much Difficulty in Introducing the ART of the Small-Sword, I almost despaired of success, and that due Esteem which so ingenious an Art deserves.
> – Blackwell, 1734: A3

Not only were wealthy students scarce, but apparently a segment of the American public felt that upper-class fencing was of little use and possibly socially disruptive to an egalitarian citizenry. In an attempt to popularize his style of fighting, Blackwell responded by outlining a six-point argument in favor of fencing, culminating in the assertion,

> But was a Man never to fight with his Sword, no Exercise is more wholesome, and delightful to the Learner, than this Fencing: For, by working all the Parts of the Body, it strengthens the Limbs, opens the Chest, gives good Air, and handsome Deportment to the Body, a majestick Tread; and makes him active, vigorous and lively; and also enables him to serve his Friend, and Country. – Blackwell, 1734: ix

The public apparently responded favorably to Blackwell's arguments as various masters in many seaboard cities established fencing schools in the colonial era. By the 19th century, uniquely American styles of fighting had developed and the cultivation of martiality as a measure of masculinity was common. Some of these American combat systems, like American-rules singlestick fighting, were based on Old World models. Others, however, were more thoroughly American. Gorn relates that in the antebellum south, where fighting was common, "gouging" or fighting with the intent of removing an opponent's eye as a symbol of victory was prevalent. To distinguish themselves from boxers and wrestlers, Southern fighters intentionally labeled their style of combat "rough and tumble" or "gouging." Gouging became a practice that was so widespread and accepted that it developed its own folklore and popular mythology (Gorn, 1985: 20–28). In other parts of the nation and among other classes, different rules of combat applied. In the "north woods," for example, "stomping" or knocking one's opponent down until he was susceptible to an attack with hob-nailed logging boots was far more prevalent and socially acceptable than gouging. In the mid-west, wrestling remained far more prominent than other forms of combative recreation leading to the development of the catch-as-catch-can style popularized by the successes of mid-western wrestlers such as a pre-presidential Abraham Lincoln (winner of a bout with the Louisiana state champion in New Salem, Louisiana in 1831) and Martin "Farmer" Burns (1861–1937), one of the first individuals to make instruction in wrestling commercially viable as a mail-order enterprise in the early part of the 20th century. Throughout the 18th and 19th centuries, as American identity was tied to the idea of the American frontier, the assertion that, "the early settlers of the frontier were the best wrestlers" became an almost self-fulfilling prophecy (although it is important to note that wrestling matches and other displays of manly arts took place at town meetings and in colleges, too) (Holliman, 1975: 149).

The American elite continued to sponsor and participate in the manly arts. Fencing and singlestick, a method of wooden sword fencing, were practiced by cadets at nearly every secondary and post-secondary military academy in the country throughout the 19th century. Theodore Roosevelt, champion of the strenuous life, advocated the practice of the manly arts for all American boys and men. As president, Roosevelt had American and Japanese instructors of wrestling, boxing, judo, and singlestick visit and practice with him at the White House. Roosevelt encouraged the practice of the traditional manly arts alongside their newer, modern athletic counterparts.[3]

By the end the 19th century, however, Americans' perceptions of the manly arts had begun to change. While the cultivation of masculinity and strength was still admired, the practice of the traditional fighting arts had begun to decline. One reason had to do with the restrictions placed on fighting in urban areas. As America became an urban nation, the behavioral excesses, eccentricities, and violence previously permitted in rural communities, accepted among male work groups such as riverboat, mining, and logging crews and even allowed within small ethnic urban communities characterized by strong social solidarity, became restricted. In urban areas, poor and working class people were confronted by elite culture, religious practices, and commercial expectations that differed significantly from their previous experience. Unable to compete materially with elites they used social behavior including dress, etiquette, and reputation to normalize relationships with supervisors, landlords, and urban officials. Practices that brought to light class and regional differences, such as participation in gouging or stomping matches, were discouraged. Furthermore, in cities with modern court systems and police forces, the recourse to personal violence to mitigate affronts was severely restricted. The editor of the online publication *Journal of Manly Arts*, Tony Wolf explains (2000: 1),

> This period [the first half of the 19th century] saw the decline of military swordplay, archery, and so-forth, concomitant with the inexorable advances of firearms and explosives. The age-old traditions of the duel of honour declined as well, and duels were eventually banned in most "civilised" countries. Towards the end of this period, many nations had established professional police forces, theoretically relieving their citizens of the need to openly carry weapons.

Other beliefs affected the practice and prevalence of the manly arts in America, as well. New theories on hygiene and disease exacerbated the decline in the practice of violent recreation. Physical contact came to be viewed as a vehicle for the transmission of disease. Contact with bodily fluids, such as blood and perspiration in the context of recreation, was particularly distasteful to many elite Americans in the Victorian-era. Elite participation and sponsorship of most traditional manly arts declined.

Fencing was the only of the archetypal manly arts that elites continued to patronize in large numbers. This was probably due to the association of fencing with a mythical Anglo-Saxon ideal and because the fencing accoutrements reasserted elites material and social primacy (Jackson-Lears, 1981: 107–140). Aldo Nadi, an Italian fencing master credited with maintaining classical martial ideals in the modern sportive era, has described fencing as unique among all contact sports stating, "Fencing is a contact sport—a contact of steel, not of fists or bodies" (Nadi, 1943: 13). In the same essay, Nadi compares fencing with boxing, concluding that fencing is physically, intellectually, and morally superior. As urbanization and the rule of law continued to discourage violent recreation in early industrial America, socially sensitive members of other classes followed the elites' lead and the appeal of bloody boxing, singlestick, and other fighting matches declined.

Nativist Americans looked askance at any form of recreation that seemed to celebrate foreign heritage. Fencing manuals, guides to the most cosmopolitan of the manly arts, were eventually rewritten to systematize and Americanize the various European fencing styles.[4] Participation in wrestling styles and boxing systems that seemed to celebrate one's immigrant heritage too strongly were seen as evidence that the practitioner was not sufficiently American. Even American styles of fighting such as catch-as-catch-can wrestling suffered as a result of their rural and regional character and their technical affinity with the Anglo-Gaelic wrestling traditions of Lancashire and Cornwall.[5]

Of the several factors that coalesced to create an atmosphere inhospitable to the practice of the traditional manly arts and favorable to the introduction of new martial sports based on the Asian martial arts in industrial-era America, the creation of modern sport weighed heavily. Modern sport and the sports ideal were disseminated from the upper and middle-classes to workers and the poor. At the same time, increasing urbanization and the concurrent rise in the fear of urban crime created a backlash against the sanitized modern sports that contributed to Americans' rapid acceptance of Asian fighting methods. Finally, widespread disillusionment with the management and practice of traditional fighting sports turned supporters of martial recreation away from the traditional manly arts even though many still had a preference for martial games, forcing them to look for new venues in which to participate in martial recreation. Concurrently, a popular, anti-modernist, nostalgic longing for the (largely mythic) pre-industrial past made American society receptive to the introduction of the Asian martial arts, particularly Japanese jujutsu and judo, which seemed to promise a sort of symbolic initiation into a universal warrior ethos. Examining the interconnected complex of these factors is the only way to explain why the Japanese martial arts were introduced, commercialized, and rapidly accepted in American society.

As the modern sport ethic developed, first among elites and Christian reformers and later among middle and working-class players, popular attitudes toward sports underwent a radical transformation.[6] Sports were transformed from celebratory, local, participatory events into codified, multi-local, and national games that were supported by hierarchical institutions regulated at levels above those occupied by most players and spectators. By the early 20th century, modern sports, as opposed to participatory games and contests, had become "the most universal aspect of popular culture" (Miller, et al., 2001: 1). One eventual result of this shift in the composition of American sport and the growth of modern athleticism was the development of a strange dichotomy among supporters of the athletic movement that pitted two views of sport against each other. On one hand, sports were seen as institutions bound by rules that limited participation and encouraged spectatorship (sowing the seeds of professionalism and commercialism). On the other hand, sports were (ideally) practiced for their own sake with the understanding that diligent practice and good sportsmanship would generate positive behavior and attributes among players off the field as well as on.

It was primarily the latter tenet, which held that sports were good for the soul as well as for the body, that encouraged sports proselytizers to cast their nets wide as they embraced games and game players outside of their upper-class circle. The rise of the new sport ethic (and its proselytizing moral accompaniment, Muscular Christianity) fostered a missionary desire to spread the sport message beyond its original race, class, and national boundaries. Both Christian and athletic missionaries carried the sports message to the far corners of the rapidly industrializing world and consequently brought it into contact with games and attitudes alien to Western upper and middle-class society. These missionary movements initially introduced the Japanese martial arts (especially a new, "scientific" martial art called judo) to the West.

By the end of the 19th century, a crisis in American sport had become apparent. Sports that were acceptable on their face to modernist athletic and Christian associations (such as the YMCA) often held little appeal for the masses that had been raised on a diet of blood sports. Those who pursued modern sports were seen as elitist and effeminate by fighting sports advocates. At the same time though, the moral justification for participating in fighting sports was usurped by sports ethicists. Therefore, those who pursued fighting sports in the tradition of the manly arts were subject to ridicule for supporting an anti-social anachronistic tradition. An unstable position prevailed in which modern athletes appeared effeminate to a significant segment of the public by their refusal to participate in martial recreation, while those who participated in fighting arts were portrayed as morally deficient. Some sports advocates worked diligently to resolve this situation by devising a sport that met modern moral criteria while it appealed to traditional, base motivations, but it was not an easily resolved issue. As late as 1946, when British boxing champion Bruce Woodcock was felled by American Tami Mauriello, sports commentator Red Smith wrote, "[Woodcock fought] like someone who learned boxing out of a book and still believes it is a manly art" (Smith, 1996: 61).

In the late 19th and early 20th centuries, participation in basketball, track and field, and bicycling flourished, but spectator patronage of those sports remained weak. At the same time, traditional bare-knuckle fighting was increasingly coming under legal censure and wrestling was beginning to show signs of becoming more show than contest. However, the public continued to patronize local (occasionally illegal) martial contests. Clearly, the manly arts still held some resonance for the American populace. Just as clearly, however, they were not going to receive the sponsorship or support that more sanitized sports enjoyed.

Asian Martial Arts Take Their Place in the U.S.A.

Sports advocates looked around the world for an activity that would meet a new set of criteria. They felt they needed an activity that held the appeal of traditional manly arts, but was free of the sordid history of boxing, free of the rural caricature that wrestling had become, and free of the elite class boundaries of fencing. They also required an activity that was modern in its approach, one that embodied the characteristics of modern sport such as regular record keeping, standardized rules, uniform entrance requirements, and norms of the industrial age (Guttman, 1978: 16). Finally, the ideal sport had to appeal not only to sports enthusiasts, but also to the general population. That meant the activity had to respond to some perceived public need such as health maintenance, the enhancement of physical appearance, or, relevant to any discussion of the manly arts, the need for self-defense. At the periphery of the Western industrial world, these sports reformers discovered a sport that met these three criteria. They discovered the Japanese grappling style called judo.

Judo was a modern synthesis of older Japanese unarmed fighting systems (jujutsu) created in 1882 by Japanese physical education specialist and jujutsu expert, Kano Jigoro. Kano had studied classical jujutsu styles but had found them unsuitable for the temperament of modern Japan and impractical for modern study.[7] Kano, a professional educator, subsequently refined the old warrior arts and organized a new systematic way of teaching the old samurai skills. Kano based his new system on two premises: that the practice of the sport had to be safe for its participants (unlike the older jujutsu styles in which practitioners were often injured) and that the sport had to appeal to practitioners of all ability levels and social classes. To increase judo's appeal within both rational, industrial society and within conservative, anti-modern circles, Kano sought to integrate modern theories on training and competition (influenced by Japanese contact with the West) with neo-traditional warrior philosophies. According to Donn Draeger and Robert Smith, "Judo tuned itself toward physical education and culture" (1980: 139). Kano even consciously planned the name of his new martial art to reflect the moral and physical characteristics he felt would popularize it as both a modern sport and a manly art. He formally called his new system *Nippon Den Kodokan Judo*, "an expression that implies 'the best budo of Japan'" (Draeger, 1996: 118). It should be noted, however, that not all of the changes initiated by Kano and his contemporaries met with unadulterated success. In *Modern Bujutsu and Budo: The Martial Ways of Japan*, one of the first rigorous reviews of the Japanese martial arts in English, the author is critical of judo and its derivatives stating, "The grappling systems are the descendants of the polytypic series of tactics that had its beginnings in the martially ineffective styles of classical jujutsu of the late Edo period" (Draeger, 1996: 60). Other martial arts, notably various styles of karate, have also been criticized for their modern emphasis on contests and the standardization of practice.[8]

From its inception, judo met the criteria that Western sports advocates sought. Judo also met most of the seven characteristics that historian Alan Guttman has stated must be present for an activity to be considered a modern sport. These characteristics encompass the sorts of changes that sports reformers had made to 19th-century Western sports such as various kinds of football and bicycle racing, characteristics that were also apparent in judo. Guttmann's criteria include secularism, equality of opportunity, the specialization of roles, rationalization, bureaucratic organization, quantification, and the quest for records (Guttman, 1978: 16). Judo has been examined in Guttmann's terms and found to meet most of these conditions. Carr determined that judo fails to qualify as a modern sport only in its relative inability to be "quantified." This, however, is a condition shared by many performance-oriented sports such as figure skating, gymnastics, and competitive dance, which suffer from subjective judging and standards and should not be seen as automatically disqualifying (Carr, 1993: 185–187).

In addition to sitting firmly in the mold of modern sport, judo also had obvious utility to urban Americans. It was a self-defense system that, theoretically at least, did not require a proponent to possess overwhelming mass or strength to overcome an opponent. It was comprised of a variety of techniques applicable under a wide variety of circumstances and could be augmented by Western fighting methods as necessary. It was reportedly safe for men, women, and children to practice and, from the outset, judo instruction in England and the United States was offered to both males and females.[9]

Judo could also be practiced easily in the limited space available in crowded industrial cities (Matsudaira, 1910: 117). Finally, judo was an intentionally moral and philosophical sport (Lindsay & Kano, 1889: 204–205; Carr, 1993: 168). Kano Jigoro consciously included instruction in moral precepts as part of the judo curriculum. Drawn from traditional Japanese philosophy and the Japanese warrior's code (*bushido*), judo philosophy contained elements that appealed directly to moral sports enthusiasts.

Those who advocated for the expansion of sporting opportunities on the basis that they contributed to moral development through the ethics of good sportsmanship and fair play observed that respect for one's opponent and self-control were cornerstones of judo practice. As a later observer noted, 19th-century sports enthusiasts believed that, "In the martial arts of Asia, conflict appears very rigid, yet consideration of the opponent is very high" (Luschen, 1981: 201). Even many Western anti-modernists, who were at best skeptical of the modern sports movement, begrudgingly accepted judo as they drew parallels between the old feudal samurai code (*bushido*) upon which judo philosophy was partially based and the legendary chivalry of English knights errant.[10]

In Japan, judo was considered one of the new-era martial ways (*shin budo*). These arts were seen as distinct from and superior to mere fighting systems because they explicitly contained a moral component. The 19th-century Japanese philosopher Aizawa Yasushi (1781–1863) stated, "To know etiquette and honor, to preserve the way of the gentleman, to strive for frugality, and thus become a bulwark of the state, is budo" (Friday, 1997: 7). While undeniably foreign to Western sports proselytizers, judo seemed to speak to a universal warrior sentiment, an idea that enjoyed widespread appeal among expansionist Americans. Furthermore, the moral codes of judo and bushido bore at least cursory similarities to the ethics championed by modern sports movement advocates. In the commentary to a lecture given to the Japan Society in 1910, Count Mutsu, a member of the Meiji government and the British Japanese Society, offered, "Our Bushido is your sportsmanship" (Matsudaira, 1910: 133). In Nitobe's *Bushido*, the 1905 English language guide to Japanese culture through its philosophical warrior tradition, chapters three through nine are titled:

    III. Rectitude or Justice

    IV. Courage, The Spirit of Daring and Bearing

    V. Benevolence, The Feeling of Distress

    VI. Politeness

    VII. Veracity and Sincerity

    VIII. Honour

    IX. The Duty of Loyalty

These chapter titles bear striking similarities to the goals espoused by organizers of the modern sports establishment who sought to instill the virtues of courage, honor, loyalty, good sportsmanship, and Christian charity in players and spectators. Early judo enthusiasts would likely have agreed with Yuasa Yasuo's (1925–2005) comment that, "Training in sports aims at developing the body's capacity.... On the other hand, the original goal in the *bushi* [warrior] way is to develop mental (or spiritual) capacity" (1993: 32).

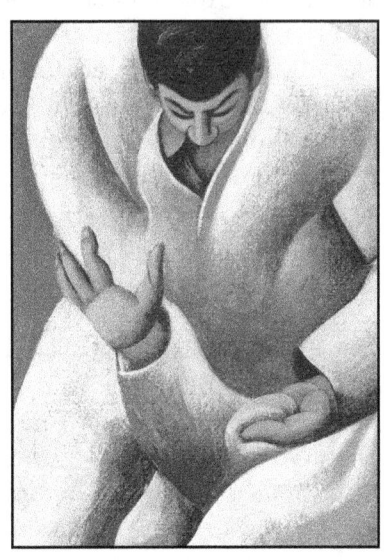

Detail of painting by Curtis Parker.

Although never popular enough to rival "American" sports like football, baseball, or even resurrected (gloved) prizefighting in the early 20th century, judo did set the stage for the introduction of other martial sports to America. From the early 20th century onward, successive "waves" of immigration of various fighting sports from around the world became nearly instantly popular only to vanish from the American public consciousness almost as quickly. Since the 1950's, East Asian martial sports with esoteric names such as Wing Chun, kempo (kenpo), ninjutsu, Muay Thai, and the syncretic martial art called Brazilian jujitsu have successively achieved popularity and commercial success in the American martial sports marketplace. American styles of fighting and American "masters" benefited from these successive waves of popularity even as they celebrated their competing martial systems as a foil to new or foreign "tricks" (Burns, 1913).

This process of acquisition, commercialization, and dissemination, begun early in American history with fencing and American styles of fighting, is characteristic of a variety of American cultural interactions. Furthermore, it addresses the situation in which "[w]e find ourselves perplexed as we try to balance winning with fair play, aggressiveness with control, freedom with technique, and the individual with community" (Hardy, 1990: 77).

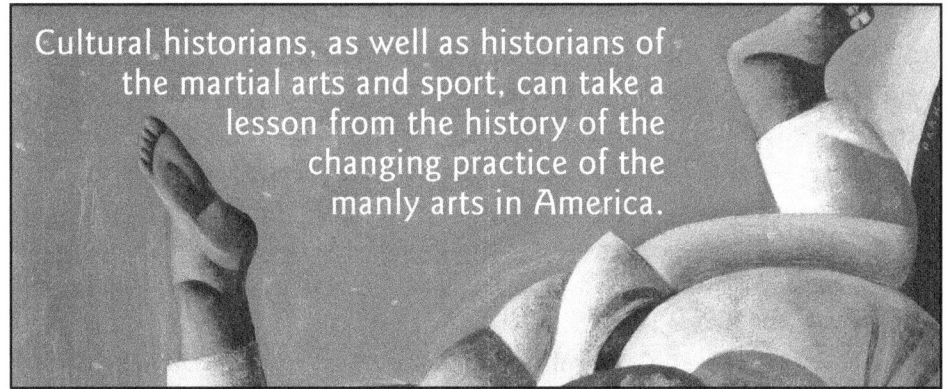

Cultural historians, as well as historians of the martial arts and sport, can take a lesson from the history of the changing practice of the manly arts in America. The continual process of adaptation and popularization apparent in the evolution of martial recreation in America from one of manly arts to modern martial sports seems to share many similarities with the American penchant for acquiring and "Americanizing" cultural institutions from around the world. Fencing, gouging, judo, and modern martial arts exist in a continuum as they integrate with and complement other aspects of American popular culture.

Endnotes

1. The two classical arguments among sports historians can be found in the works of Mandell and Sansone. Mandell (1984) argues that sport is a cultural complement to industrialism. Sansone (1988) maintains that sports are the modern expression of the universal human struggle with contest and cooperation.
2. Most of the hundreds of summaries of judo history available paraphrase the account provided in Lindsay and Kano (1889: 192–205). Judo's history and development have been treated at length in a variety of sources, notably in English in Draeger (1974/1996: 112–123). The integration of judo into British popular culture is described in Wingard (2003: 16–25).
3. The most thorough description of Roosevelt's martial activities is found in Donovan (1909). For a more complete analysis of the implications of Roosevelt's participation in martial sports on the man and the arts in America see Burdick (1999: 22–54).
4. See Cass (1930: 17–18), for an example of a consciously Americanized fencing manual.
5. For an example of the continuing dissemination and adaptation of Anglo-Gaelic wrestling in 20th-century U.S.A., see Pittman (1999: 48–57), specifically pp.

49 and 57.

[6] Some works that treat the rise of modern sports in great detail include Guttmann (1978) and Holt (1989).

[7] In 1868, the Meiji emperor wrested control of Japan away from the last Tokugawa shogun. To solidify his position and assert control over conservative samurai, the emperor embarked on a course to rapidly modernize Japan. Many trappings of the old regime were outlawed and others quickly fell into disuse. Some martial arts changed their curricula to appeal to more popular audiences. An archetypal discussion of the symbolic character and implication of these changes to Japanese martial culture is included in Funakoshi Gichin's memoir (1975: 1–7).

[8] Recently, scholarly examinations of judo's early years of have been published with increasing frequency, including Gray Carr (1993: 167–188), Smith (1996: 60–65), and Bowen (1999: 43–53).

[9] Barton-Wright (1902: 261–264) and Norman (1905) both exalt the suitability of judo and related exercises across class, race, and gender boundaries.

[10] It is important to note that the Japanese warrior ideal the English admired was a concept largely derived from Nitobe (1905) and by pamphlets published by Westerners residing for short periods in Japan (e.g. Norman (1905: 1–3). Nitobe had been educated in English public schools and was Christian. It is likely that his version of the samurai honor code was highly idealized, if not specifically coordinated to appeal to an English audience. Similarly the pamphleteers' accounts must also be viewed critically as their motives were frequently commercial or evangelical.

References

Barton-Wright, E.W. (1902). Ju-jitsu and Ju-do. *Transactions and proceedings of the Japan Society*, London 5: 261–264.

Blackwell, E. (1734). *A compleat system of fencing: Or, the art of defence*. Williamsburg: William Parks.

Bowen, R. (1999). Origins of the British Judo Association, the European Judo Union & the International Judo Federation. *Journal of Asian Martial Arts*, 8(3): 43–53.

Burdick, D. (1999). The American way of fighting: Unarmed defense in the United States, 1845–1945. Ph.D. Dissertation, University of Indiana.

Burns, M. (1913). *Jiu Jitsu–Self defense and their relation to wrestling: Lesson XII* (Book VI). Omaha: Farmer Burns School of Wrestling.

Carr, K. (1993). Making way: War, philosophy and sport in Japanese judo. *Journal of Sport History*, 20(2): 167–188.

Cass, E. (1930). *The book of fencing*. Boston: Lothrop, Lee and Shepard, Co.

Donovan, M. (1909). *The Roosevelt that I know: Ten years of boxing with the president – and other memories of famous men*. New York: B.W. Dodge and Co.

Draeger, D. (1996). *Modern bujutsu and budo: The martial arts and ways of Japan.* New York: Weatherhill.

Draeger, D. & R. Smith. (1980). *Comprehensive Asian fighting arts.* New York: Kodansha International.

Dykhuizen, J. (2000): Culture, training and perception of the martial arts: Aikido's example. *Journal of Asian Martial Arts,* 9(3): 9–31.

Friday, K. (1997). *Legacies of the sword: The Kashima-Shinryu and samurai martial culture.* Honolulu: University of Hawai'i Press.

Funakoshi, G. (1975). *Karate-do, my way of life.* New York: Kodansha International.

Gorn, E. (1985). Gouge and bite, pull hair and scratch: The social significance of fighting in the southern backcountry. *American Historical Quarterly,* 90(1): 18–43.

Gray, W. Russel. (1987). For whom the bell tolled: The decline of British prize fighting in the Victorian era. *Journal of Popular Culture,* 21(2): 53–64.

Guttmann, A. (1978). *From ritual to record: The nature of modern sports.* New York: Columbia University Press.

Holliman, J. (1975). American sports 1785–1835. No. 34 of Perspectives in American History. Philadelphia: Porcupine Press.

Holt, R. (1989). *Sport and the British: A modern history.* Oxford: Clarendon Press.

Hardy, S. (1990). Entrepreneurs, structures and sportgeist. In *Essays on Sport History and Sport Mythology,* edited by Donald Kyle and Gary Stark. College Station: Texas A&M University Press.

Jackson-Lears, T. (1981). *No place of grace: Anti-modernism and the transformation of American culture 1880–1920.* New York: Pantheon Books.

Jones, H. (1943). *Judo, jiu-jitsu, and hand-to-hand fighting: A list of references.* Washington, D.C.: The Library of Congress Division of Bibliography.

Lindsay, T. & J. Kano (1889). Jiujutsu the old samurai art of fighting without weapons, *Transactions of the Asiatic Society of Japan,* 16: 192–205.

Luschen, G. (1981). The system of sport—Problems of methodology, conflict and social stratification. In *Handbook of the Social Science of Sport,* edited by Gunther Luschen and George Sage. Champaign, IL: Stipes Publishing Co.

Mandell, R. (1984). *Sport: A cultural history.* New York: Columbia University Press.

Matsudaira, T. (1910). Sports and physical training in modern Japan. *Transactions and proceedings of the Japan Society,* London, 8: 114–134.

Miller, T., G. Lawrence, J. McCay & D. Rowe. (2001). *Globalization and sport: Playing the world.* London: Sage Publications.

Nadi, A. (1943). *On fencing.* New York: G.P Putnam's Son.

Nitobe, I. (1905). *Bushido.* New York: G.P. Putnam's Sons.

Norman, F. (1905). *The righting man of Japan, the training and exercises of the samurai.* London: Archibald Constable & Co. Ltd.

Pittman, A. (1999). Combat wrestling: Geoghan's blend from East and West. *Journal of Asian Martial Arts,* 8(4): 48–57.

Sansone, D. (1988). *Greek athletics and the genesis of sport.* Berkeley: University of California Press.

Sidmore, M. (1995). Oriental contributions to Western popular culture: The martial arts. *Journal of Popular Culture, 25*(1): 129–148.

Smith, R. (1996). The masters contest of 1926: An epiphany in judo history. *Journal of Asian Martial Arts, 5*(3): 60–65.

Wingard, G. (2003). Sport, industrialism and the Japanese gentle way: Judo in late Victorian England. *Journal of Asian Martial Arts, 12*(2): 16–25.

Wolf, T. (2000). An introduction to the Journal of Manly Arts. *Electronic Journals of Martial Arts and Sciences: Journal of Manly Arts,* http://ejmas.com/jmanly/jmanlymission.htm (17 February, 2003).

Yuasa, Y. (1993). *The body, self-cultivation, and ki energy.* New York: State University of New York Press.

Judo Comes to California
Judo vs. Wrestling in the American West, 1900–1920

by Matt Hlinak, M.A., J.D.

Left side: kanji script for "judo" and "jujutsu".
Photograph of George Hackenschmidt (1878–1968),
the first recognized World Heavyweight
Wrestling Champion in 1905.

Introduction

This essay analyzes Japanese-American immigration into the American West through the prism of athletics, specifically by examining a series of contests between Japanese-American *judoka* (practitioners of judo) and European-American wrestlers from 1900 to 1920 in California. The popularity of these matches demonstrates the complex relationship between Japanese-Americans and the dominant European-American culture of the western states during this period.

This complexity will be shown first by looking at the way in which martial arts are closely linked to national and ethnic identity. During the latter half of the 1800s, the western martial arts of boxing and wrestling began the trend toward internationalization of sport which led to the first modern Olympic Games in 1896. Nationalism in sport followed almost immediately behind. The American style of "catch wrestling" evolved from European wrestling styles shaped by nineteenth-century notions of fair play and the manly arts. Significantly, early catch wrestlers honed their craft traveling with carnivals throughout the country, cultivating a backwoods sense of competition and masculinity. While professional wrestling has devolved into "muscular theater" today, wrestlers in the *fin de siècle* West were viewed as paragons of rough-and-tumble frontier masculinity.

Similarly, judo held an important position in Japanese society. Unlike American catch wrestling, with its origins in various European folk wrestling styles, judo is an entirely indigenous Japanese martial art. In an effort to prove the effectiveness of their art, a handful of skilled judoka traveled around the world, challenging (and often defeating) local wrestlers; these successes led many Japanese to equate judo with Japan's recent rise in global political and economic stature. Similarly, many westerners saw the mysterious art of judo as an explanation for Japan's seemingly inexplicable military victory over Russia in the Russo-Japanese War (1904–05). Japanese immigrants to the western United States brought judo with them and the sport quickly gained popularity with European-Americans.

Not all of the responses were positive, however. Many westerners simply dismissed judo based on perceptions of racial inferiority of Japanese. Others criticized judo's tactics, finding them inconsistent with the evolving ideals of western sportsmanship. But many European-American admired the way in which a skilled judoka could defeat a significantly larger opponent, and a few even attributed mystical or supernatural abilities to athletes of Japanese origin.

A strong barnstorming tradition existed in both judo and catch wrestling, so conflict between the two was inevitable. Matches pitting judoka against wrestlers almost always earned higher billing than matches featuring two competitors of the same style. They also spawned numerous essays in western newspapers comparing the two martial arts.

This chapter will conclude with a discussion of why these matches were so appealing to European-Americans in the western states. One reason was a simple interest in Japanese culture. But European-Americans also enjoyed the way in which these matches reinforced stereotypes about Japanese-Americans. For example, a judoka's ability to defeat a larger opponent emphasized the supposed smaller physical stature of Japanese people. Judoka were also portrayed as excessively polite, in contrast to the rugged western wrestlers, which presented contrasting notions of masculinity. Similarly, judo techniques that would be illegal in a western wrestling match were viewed as dirty tactics inconsistent with gentlemanly sporting traditions. In the eyes of European-Americans, judo, like the Japanese themselves, was an alien concept to be alternatively ridiculed and feared.

Much of the European-American interest in these matches arose out of anxiety over the larger socio-political context. Westerners felt threatened by Asian immigration as well as Japan's increasing military and economic power. These matches allowed them to vicariously act out their anxiety. For this reason, we continue to see racial match-ups in professional wrestling to this day. Indeed, legitimate sports today are contested in an atmosphere of subtle and not-so-subtle nationalism and even outright racism. By understanding the historical basis for the darker elements of athletics, modern competitors and fans may be able to conquer these elements and simply enjoy the match.

Announcement of bout between
Adolph "Ad" Santal (above) and
jujutsu expert Tarra Mikania.
Los Angeles Times (7 April 1915).

A Note on Terminology

Throughout this work, the terms "judo" and "jujutsu" will be used interchangeably, although they are not synonymous. As will be discussed in greater detail in Part I, judo evolved from jujutsu, a process which began with the formation of Kano Jigaro Kodokan academy in 1882 and culminated in judo's debut as an Olympic sport at the 1964 Summer Games in Tokyo. During this transitional period, judo was often viewed simply as the particularly effective form of jujutsu practiced by Kano and his students, but not as a distinct martial art. The majority of *jujutsuka* (practitioners of jujutsu) discussed herein trace their martial arts lineage back to Kano, so it is not inaccurate to refer to them as judoka. More importantly, however, the rather ill-defined distinction between judo and jujutsu would not have been understood by the European-American journalists who produced much of the primary source material relied upon here. No attempt will therefore be made to attempt to discern whether a particular athlete considered himself a student of judo or jujutsu (Burdick, 1999; Carr, 1993; Shun, 1998).

While "judo" and "jujutsu" will be used more broadly than would be accurate, the term "wrestling" will be used more narrowly than it is often construed. The *American Heritage Dictionary* defines wrestling as, "[a] sport in which two competitors attempt to throw or immobilize each other by grappling," which would include both judo and jujutsu. In this work, "wrestling" will refer only to European-based grappling styles in which the goal is to pin the opponent's shoulders to the mat, rather than to cause the opponent to concede the match ("submit") by means of chokeholds or joint manipulation as in jujutsu-inspired martial arts. Western wrestling styles satisfying this definition will also be discussed in greater detail in Part I.

I. Martial Arts and National Identity

Wrestling and American Culture

Wrestling in the United States evolved from a number of European-based wrestling styles, particularly those of British origin. In the Cumberland and Westmorland style, competitors locked their arms around one another (a position known to modern wrestlers as "the clinch") and the loser was the first to break his grip. Wrestlers in the Cornish-style wore jackets, which were held in order to gain an advantage as in modern judo. Devonshire-style wrestling was similar to Cornish-style except it also allowed kicking to the shins. One of the most influential styles was Irish collar-and-elbow wrestling, in which competitors began by gripping one another by the collar and elbow; this form spread rapidly through the Northern states during the Civil War due to the large numbers of Irish immigrants in the Union armies. French, German, Dutch, African, and Native American wrestling styles further influenced the development of a uniquely American wrestling style (Archer & Svinth, 2005; Gorn, 1985; Morton & O'Brien, 1985; Pope, 1997; Savenga, 1995).

Wrestling played an important role in American culture in the nineteenth century. The sport found its way into "American folklore from the early days of Republic up to the Civil War" through "tales of the wrestling prowess of its men" (Morton & O'Brien 1985: 19–20). George Washington and Abraham Lincoln both garnered considerable acclaim for their grappling skills, while wrestlers featured prominently in the works of Mark Twain. Competitions between soldiers during the Civil War followed by post-war urbanization led to standardizing rules and techniques—with some resistance (see Guttmann, 1994)—into a style known as "catch-as-catch-can" or catch wrestling, which made it possible to pit champions from one locality against one another. This standardization, coupled with a strong interest in betting on matches, allowed wrestlers to evolve from rural strongmen into the nation's first professional athletes. While baseball would grow to become the national pastime, its development as a professional sport lagged significantly behind wrestling in the latter decades of the 1800s. At the peak of wrestling's popularity in 1911, more than 35,000 fans packed into Chicago's Comiskey Park to watch the rematch between Frank Gotch (1878–1917)— "one of America's earliest athletic superstars" (Hewitt, 2005: 13–14)—and Georg Hackenschmidt (1878–1968); the live gate for the bout came to $87,000, or over 1.8 million in today's dollars (Betts, 1974; Fielding, 1975; Fielding, 1977; Hewitt, 2005; Rickard, 1999).

Frank Gotch, two-time
victor over G. Hackenschmidt
in 1908 and 1911.

But wrestling was not merely popular in the United States; it was a distinctly American endeavor, one that resonated with the frontier culture of the western states. A number of commentators have described the sport in this time period using the language of the borderlands. Morton & O'Brien (1985: 9, 20) note that "[r]ecords of American westward expansion are replete with descriptions of one-eyed brawlers, earless innkeepers, and others who bore scars from pankration ['a no-holds barred combination of boxing and wrestling'] bouts". Hewitt (2005: 1–2) describes a "rough-and-tumble fighting tradition long associated with the frontier [in which] [b]ackwoodsmen regularly engaged in anything-goes brawling….". Archer & Svinth (2005) place wrestlers at home in the quintessentially borderlands environs of "saloons, Wild West shows and circuses, and vaudeville."

Contemporary writers similarly viewed wrestling as an endeavor closely tied to American culture. Journalists of the pre-World War I era routinely made reference to the "All American" sport of wrestling (LAT, December 18, 1914), "the American method of catch-as-catch-can" (OT, August 29, 1905), or "the Yankee plan" of self-defense (LAT, March 4, 1905). The "American method" was a popular and thoroughly western sport in the United States at the dawn of the twentieth century.

Judo and Japanese Culture

All cultures in the world have participated in some form of grappling since before recorded history, and the Japanese are no exception. The precursors to jujutsu developed in the medieval period as a means of combat for samurai who found themselves without their swords. Because the striking techniques found in other Asian martial arts would be ineffective against a heavily-armored opponent, the samurai created a fighting style which would allow them to immobilize an opponent with limited use of punches or kicks. A style which would be recognizable to a modern jujutsuka took shape in the 1600s. While jujutsu's origins can be traced to the battlefield, it was a prolonged period of peace in the seventeenth and eighteenth centuries which caused the martial art to flourish. In the absence of war, jujutsu became the sole means by which members of the warrior class could demonstrate their masculinity, particularly as the government steadily eroded the privileges once held by the samurai. As jujutsu became increasingly divorced from its battlefield origins, the style abandoned many practical techniques in favor of those which were aesthetically pleasing (Burdick, 1997; Carr, 1993).

Founder of judo,
Kano Jigoro (1860–1938).
Photo from the Kodokan.

During this era of peace, the Tokugawa government kept Japan largely isolated from the rest of the world. In 1853, Commodore Matthew Perry of the United States Navy threatened Japan with military intervention if it did not open its ports to American merchant vessels. The humiliating 1858 Treaty of Amity and Commerce put an end to Japanese isolationism. This abrupt "opening" of the island nation shook Japanese society, causing simultaneous and contradictory pushes towards both tradition and modernity. Many Japanese clung to their traditional social customs, like jujutsu, in the face of American and European cultural invasion, while also striving to adopt the western military and economic systems which had made the influx of foreigners possible. It was against this socio-political backdrop that Kano Jigoro founded the Kodokan, his jujutsu academy in Tokyo (Burdick, 1997; Guttmann, 1994; Guttmann & Thompson, 2001; Rosenblum, 1981).

Kano very much typified the modernist/traditionalist dichotomy of late nineteenth century Japan. Born two years after the Treaty of Amity and Commerce, Kano was a student of western philosophers like John Stuart Mill and Herbert

Spencer, as well as traditional Japanese jujutsu. Many martial arts schools at this time were, in Kano's view, overly reliant on ritual and aesthetics with insufficient emphasis on practical techniques, while other schools gave jujutsu a bad name by training ruffians who studied the art to make themselves more proficient street-fighters and muggers. His goal was to make jujutsu both more practical and more gentlemanly. In effect, he wanted to create a sport, which he did by gathering together those traditions he found useful and by abandoning those he found lacking (Burdick, 1997; Carr, 1993; Guttmann, 1994; Guttmann & Thompson, 2001; Kiku, 2004; Shun, 1998; Svinth, 2003).

"Jap Jiu Jitsu" experts to appear at the Los Angeles Athletic Club in 1913. Illustration from the *Los Angeles Times* (7 April 1913).

Kano called his style Kodokan judo to distinguish his methods from other forms of jujutsu. The Tokyo Metropolitan Police Bureau periodically held jujutsu competitions in part to select instructors for training officers. As the Kodokan consistently defeated representatives from other schools, the resulting publicity caused Kano's student body to grow from ten students in 1884, to nearly 500 in 1887, to an astounding 2,755 in 1892. As Kano's students founded their own schools throughout Japan and the world, the practice of judo spread exponentially (Burdick, 1999; Carr, 1993; Shun, 1998).

The rise of judo did not occur in a vacuum, however. A strong nationalist movement was also taking hold in Japan. While Kano himself was not particularly conservative, his philosophy of fusing modernity and tradition struck a chord with the ruling élite who wanted to use modern western methods to bring traditional Japanese culture onto the world stage. In an effort to distance himself from some of the rougher elements which had been associated with jujutsu, Kano enforced a code of conduct which mirrored the bushido of the samurai. At the same time, the Japanese government was attempting to revive elements of samurai culture in order to restore national pride after the Treaty of Amity and Commerce. Judo quickly earned government support due to the combination of its effectiveness against other art forms and its seeming shared values with nationalist politics. By 1911, the Japanese Ministry of Education added judo to the national physical education curriculum. Many Japanese felt that judo was the institution that best represented Japan's rise from humiliation to power in the latter half of the nineteenth century (Burdick, 1999; Guttmann & Thompson, 2001; Shun, 1998).

While judo played a significant role in Japanese society during this period, many European-Americans viewed it as a virtually essential element of the culture. Contemporary American accounts were full exaggerated claims. One author proclaimed the entire nation of Japan, "from the emperor down to the humblest coolie," practiced judo (CRH, July 21, 1904). Even among immigrants, it was felt, "[t]here is not a Japanese in Los Angeles who doesn't know enough about the art to defend himself more than successfully against any man not of his own race" (LAT, February 18, 1918). Another rather bizarre article claims "the hardy little Jap, who is the embodiment of 'wiriness' and who seems incapable of fatigue, though his sustenance is only a few grains of rice," attains this superhuman endurance from the study of jujutsu, which requires such "daily habits" as bathing twice a day "if [the jujutsuka] would imitate his Japanese teachers" and drinking "a gallon of pure water" (SFC, March 27, 1904). While there was a good bit of journalistic exaggeration taking place in these articles, the sport enjoyed great popularity with Japanese-Americans as both participants and spectators (Svinth, 2003).

European-American Views of Judo

Due to an influx of Japanese immigrants from 1884–1907, European-Americans gained an interest in Japanese culture. Newspapers in this era spent much time explaining the mysterious art of judo to white audiences. These early accounts tended to fall into two extreme categories, dismissal and admiration. The most laughable of the former category simply argued that European-Americans were culturally and physiologically superior to Japanese- Americans, therefore American sports like wrestling and boxing must be superior to judo. In one representative account, an editorial in the *Oakland Tribune* argued, "a finished catch-as-catch can artist would be more than a match for any Jiu Jitsu enthusiasts for the reason that his science embraces the art of protection, which in conjunction with his native American aggressiveness, would be practically invulnerable" (OT, August 29, 1905). A writer for *Harper's Weekly* opined, "the Japanese temperament is uncertain and changeful…given to sudden flights and sudden flagging," and felt Japanese athletes possessed, "that notable deficiency of all Orientals, the lack of steadfastness and perseverance" (HW, February 12, 1898). The *Los Angeles Times* declared, "it would not take the average man very long to guess that a good boxer would make the best judo wrestler look like 20 cents worth of dog meat" (LAT, December 26, 1909). Another article described "jew-joot" as "a humbug the American people should be ashamed to fool with, and that any ordinary white man can make the brown chap lie down" (LAT, May 7, 1905). Spelling the first syllable of the word jujutsu as "jew" was fairly common in articles criticizing the Japanese style (see, e.g., MAB, June 1905); this was likely an attempt to denigrate Asian culture by appealing to existing anti-Semitic sentiment in the United States (Burdick, 1999; Wilson, 2000).

Other writers in the dismissal camp at least based their opinions on actual contests in which European-Americans defeated judoka. In these cases, headlines emphasized the race of the competitors rather than their fighting styles, such as, "Cadets Down the 'Jap'" (NYT, February 21, 1905) and "American Floors Victorious Jap" (LAT, March 4, 1905).

Some European-Americans continued to dismiss judo even when judoka defeated American wrestlers. As western sports standardized in the late nineteenth century, boxing and wrestling adopted rules to prevent injury and to help "civilize" the European immigrants who practiced these sports (Burdick, 1999). Judo allowed the use of chokes and joint-locks which were not permitted in western wrestling styles, such that "[m]any of the tricks employed by the little brown man would be scorned as 'foul' by our exponents of the manly art" (SFC, October 16, 1904). The *Los Angeles Times* described, "Judo or third degree business" as "'rough stuff' pure and simple" (LAT, December 26, 1909). One commentator summarized the criticism of judo techniques by declaring "[a]ny audience fond of fair play would brand them as fouls, and after their first appearance they would be ruled as unfair advantages" (Terry, 1902, quoted in Burdick, 1999).

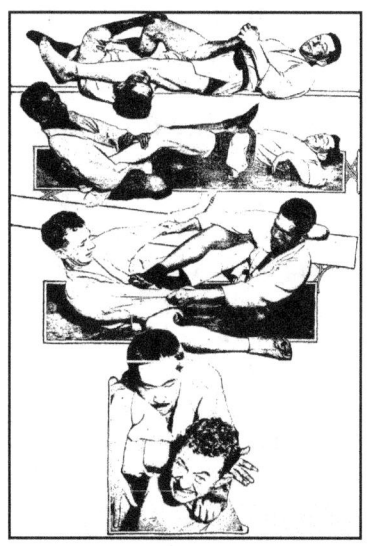

Pat Higgins and Ito Tokugoro at practice. *Los Angeles Times* (24 October 1916).

Other European-Americans, including President Theodore Roosevelt, were great admirers of judo (Burdick, 1999). Of particular interest to western audiences was the way in which judo could be used by a smaller man, or even a woman (see Svinth, 2000b; Svinth, 2001), to defeat a larger opponent. The *Salt Lake Herald* noted "a small Jap versed in [judo's] mysteries can easily overcome the largest athletes trained only in wrestling or boxing" (SLH, February 5, 1906). Indeed, "[t]he science of Jiu jitsu teaches the athlete to make the other man use his strength against himself, and once a little man gets a hold his larger opponent inflicts greater punishment upon himself by resisting because of his great size" (SFC, December 17, 1907). This ability was attributed to "the well-known mechanical principle of the lever" along with "the obvious result of the application of mechanical laws and strategic means" (LAT, September 4, 1904).

Other commentators attributed judo's efficacy to the quasi-supernatural abilities of its practitioners. Judoka were reported to be able to use "vital touches" against an opponent's "death points," the location of which were closely-guarded secrets, in order to cause "a temporary paralysis of the arm to the complete suspension of vital processes and instant death" (LAT, September 4, 1904). One judoka was "credited with a way of looking at an opponent that causes all the symptoms of painter's colic and some of his great victories have been won via mental grapevine" (LAT, April 3, 1919). There was even a fear that those Japanese-Americans who opened judo schools hid from their European-American students certain mysterious techniques which would come into play in some future conflict between Japan and the United States (Burdick, 1999).

II. The Barnstormers

As Japanese immigrants integrated into American society, contests between Japanese-American judoka and European-American wrestlers were inevitable. Both sports had strong barnstorming traditions. Professional wrestlers of this era were often carnival employees who took on local champions as the circus traveled from town to town. Wrestlers were therefore predisposed towards challenging athletes from other localities in order to prove their skills. Similarly, judo's popularity in Japan arose out of Kano Jigoro's desire to prove his style superior to other schools of jujutsu. It is no surprise that his students engaged in similar contests after immigrating to the United States (Burdick, 1999; Carr, 1993; Hewitt, 2005; Morton & O'Brien, 1985; Shun, 1998).

The earliest bouts were more or less inconclusive as the wrestler was generally able to take down and pin his opponent while the judoka was likewise able to throw and submit his; the result was therefore dependent upon which sport's rules were applied. Later bouts were contested under hybrid rules systems, which effectively leveled the playing field. There were at least forty major

Ito Tokugoro, jujutsu wrestler extraordinaire. Images from the *Seattle Post-Intelligencer*, (6 November 6, 1909).

judoka/wrestler bouts that took place between 1904 and 1920, and almost three-quarters of these took place west of the Mississippi River. San Francisco catch wrestler Adolph "Ad" Santel (1887–1966) ran up a number of victories over judoka which led him to proclaim himself the judo champion of the world. Seattle judoka Ito Tokugoro gained the attention of European-American fans after notching victories over several prominent wrestlers, including Eddie Robinson and Ted Thye. Santel and Ito met twice in San Francisco in 1916; Santel won the first bout after Ito's head struck the floor, rendering him unable to continue (Burdick, 1999; Hewitt, 2005; Svinth, 2003). In the re-match, "Santell [sic] gave a couple of gurgles, turned black in the face and thumped the floor, signifying he'd had enough" of Ito's chokehold (LAT, February 1, 1917).

These mixed matches were tremendously popular, consistently earning higher billing and receiving greater media attention than wrestler vs. wrestler or judoka vs. judoka matches. In particular, these contests seemed to appeal to fans that rooted for competitors based on race. A Japanese-American judoka was cheered on by "a crowd of jabbering Japanese enthusiasts" (LAT, December 9, 1917), while in another contest "[t]he white element tried hard to make as much noise as the Japs, but the brown men howled continually" (LAT, May 31, 1909). In one match, "the white people" — including the unabashedly partisan sportswriter — "shouted for the white man and we did all that we could to make him win, but the Japs outnumbered us and they outdid us in the matter of enthusiasm" (OT, April 2, 1909). When a lone European-American woman, "a certain ordinary-looking person who was dressed as a lady" — the implication of course being that such a woman could not actually be a "lady" — lent her support to a Japanese-American judoka, "it called forth the cat calls and hisses of the house and the things that were said about this certain young person would not look well in print." Not only did most fans choose their loyalties based upon race, but those that failed to do so could find themselves subject to harassment by spectators and even insults by journalists.

III. What Was the Appeal of These Matches?

European-Americans were interested in judoka/wrestler matches for a number of reasons. One was a simple interest in Japanese culture. After all, Japan had until only recently been closed to westerners, so the exposure to judo gave a glimpse into the society that produced it. But European-Americans also enjoyed the way in which these matches reinforced stereotypes about Japanese-Americans. For example, a judoka's ability to defeat a larger opponent emphasized the supposed smaller physical stature of Japanese people. Thus, even when praising the skill of a judoka, European-American journalists would dismissively refer to him as a "hardy little Jap" (SFC, March 27, 1904) or "little brown gentleman" (LAT, February 18, 1918). In addition, some journalists seem to delight in quoting, often at length, the broken English of immigrant judoka in order to present them

Ito Tokugoro, "the worlds greatest jiu-jitsu and judo expert, who threw Ad Santell and is the idol of his countrymen."
Los Angeles Times (1 February 1917).

as less intelligent than native speakers (see, e.g., LAT, April 3, 1919). Judoka were also portrayed as excessively polite, in contrast to the rough-and-tumble western wrestlers, which presented contrasting notions of masculinity. One is described as an "inoffensive fellow" while another "smiled and maintained his good humor" throughout a rough match (Edgren, 1905). Respectful judo competitors are depicted "formally kowtowing to each other," while when "American boys wrestle, they do it in an impromptu and rather reckless fashion which would shock the convention-bound Jap" (ST, March 10, 1907). In another account, a *judogi* (judo uniform) was referred to as "a jaunty Japanese nightie" and the judoka as "a saucy little bantam" up against a "husky white man" (LAT, December 9, 1917). Regardless of the outcome of the bout, the reader was left with no doubt who the "real man" in the contest was (see also Sabo, 1985).

As the modern nation-state is a relatively recent phenomenon, so to is nationalism, which can be defined "as a condition of mind, feeling, or sentiment of a group of people living in a well-defined geographical area, speaking a common language, possessing a literature in which the aspirations of the nation have been expressed, and, in some cases, having a common religion" (Snyder, 1990). The regrettable flipside to the communal good feelings towards other members of the state takes the form of racism and xenophobia towards those living outside the state; if nationalism instills in us a belief that our culture is superior, other cultures must therefore by inferior. In the wake of the Civil War, American nationalism was on the rise. This nationalism often took the form of what Billig (1995) terms "banal nationalism," which includes routine expressions of nationalist sentiment, such as children's recitation of the Pledge of Allegiance before school or the use of patriotic symbols on postage stamps and currency. Banal nationalism found routine expression in sporting contests of the day "as the nation was 'represented' in competition short of war" (McCrone, 1998). Athletes in international competition embody the state and their successes and failures are shared by their fellow citizens (Betts, 1974; Copeci & Wilkerson, 1983; Germs, 2006; Guttmann, 1988; Guttman, 1994; Hobsbawn, 1990; Loy & Elvogue, 1970; Kiku, 2004; Mandell, 1984; Mogull, 1981; Mrozek, 1983; Pope, 1997; Rainville et al., 1978; Schneider & Eitzen, 1979).

Much of the European-American interest in these matches arose out of anxiety over the larger socio-political context. Westerners felt threatened by Japanese immigration, which was effectively shut off by a 1907 "gentleman's agreement" between President Roosevelt and the Japanese government. Japanese-Americans, even those of the second generation, were denied citizenship under the Naturalization Act of 1790, which only applied to "free white persons." More locally, the California Alien Land Law of 1913 barred Asian-Americans from owning real property. Despite these restrictions against Japanese-Americans, western laborers still feared an influx of low-paid, foreign workers. Similarly, Japan's 1905 military victory over Russia, the first victory by an Asian power over a European country, gave rise to fears of Japanese imperialism (Burdick, 1999; Germs, 2006; Wilson, 2000). In fact, many in the West attributed Japan's victory to the study of judo; one writer went so far as to recommend the study of jujutsu "for Anglo-Saxon readers" so that "peace congresses will soon be a thing of the past" (SFC, October 16, 1904).

In order to understand how these socio-political anxieties influenced sports fans during this period, it is useful to look at studies of modern professional wrestling, which, it should be noted, is far more theatrical than the early twentieth century judoka/wrestler matches (many of which were legitimate athletic contests). Modern professional wrestling fans "are low income workers, welfare recipients, or immigrants who are finding little success in what is supposed to be the land of opportunity" and enjoy the vicarious thrills of "sports entertainment" (Campbell, 1996). These groups are particularly interested in storylines in which a "foreign menace" reflecting a current military or economic threat to the United States is defeated by an American hero, who is almost always of European descent. Ethnicity is often used to distinguish "good guys" from "bad guys." European-American wrestling fans of the pre-World War I era would likely have felt similar motivations, particularly due to the tense political and economic climate in which they lived. Moreover, the fact that the athletic contests they watched had at least the perception of legitimacy, they may have invested more emotionally in their support of a favorite athlete as opposed to modern fans who know they are watching "muscular theater" (Archer & Svinth, 2005; Mondak, 1989; Deeter-Schmeltz & Sojka, 2004).

Conclusion

The contests between wrestling and judo in the first two decades of the twentieth century show an American West that is both intrigued by and in fear of Japanese-Americans and the burgeoning power of their native land. Much of these sentiments were expressed in an ugly nationalism, which is fortunately absent—at least in such obvious terms—from modern political dialogue. But nationalism and even racism remain driving forces in modern sports, where many of our more cosmopolitan instincts are drowned out in the heat of battle. By better understanding the origins of these forces, we may achieve the Olympian goal of truly casting aside cultural differences in the name of athletic competition.

Bibliography

Archer, J. & Svinth, J. (2005). Professional wrestling: Where sport and theater collide. *InYo: Journal of Alternative Perspectives*. Available: http://web.archive.org/web/20070818163456/ejmas.com/jalt/jaltframe.htm.

Betts, J. (1971). Home front, battlefield and sport during the Civil War. *Research Quarterly* 42: 113–32.

Betts, J. (1974). *America's sporting heritage: 1850–1950*. Reading, MA: Addison-Wesley Publishing Co.

Billig, M. (1995). *Banal nationalism*. London: Sage Publications.

Burdick, D. (1999). *The American way of fighting: Unarmed defense in the United States, 1845–1945*. Doctoral dissertation, Indiana University, Bloomington.

Campbell, J. (1996). Professional wrestling: Why the bad guy wins. *Journal of American Culture* 19(2): 127–132.

Carr, K. (1993). Making way: War, philosophy and sport in Japanese judo. *Journal of Sport History* 20(2): 167–188.

Copeci, D. & Wilkerson, M. (1983). Multifarious hero. *Journal of Sport History* 10(3), 5–25.

Deeter-Schmelz, D. & Sojka, J. (2004). Wrestling with American values: An exploratory investigation of World Wrestling Entertainment as a product-based subculture. *Journal of Consumer Behaviour* 4(2): 132–143.

Edgren, R. (1905). The fearful art of jiu jitsu. *Outing*, 322–28. Reprinted in Svinth, J. (ed.) (2000). *Journal of Combative Sport*. Available: http://ejmas.com/jcs/jcsart_edgren1_0300.htm.

Fielding, L. (1975). Reflections from the sport mirror: selected treatments of Civil War sport. *Journal of Sport History* 2: 132–144.

Fielding, L. (1977). War and trifles: sport in the shadow of Civil War Army life. *Journal of Sport History* 4: 151–168.

FILA (2004). *History of wrestling. International Wrestling Hall of Fame*. Available: http://www.filahalloffame.com/historyofwrestling.html.

Germs, G. (2006). *The athletic crusade: Sport and American cultural imperialism*. Lincoln, NE: University of Nebraska Press.

Gorn, E. (1985). "Gouge and bite, pull hair and scratch": The social significance of fighting in the southern backcountry. *American Historical Review* 90(1): 18–43.

Guttmann, A. (1988). *A whole new ball game: an interpretation of American sports*. Chapel Hill: University of North Carolina Press.

Guttmann, A. (1994). *Games and empires: Modern sports and cultural imperialism*. New York: Columbia University Press.

Guttmann, A. & Thompson, L. (2001). *Japanese sports: A history*. Honolulu: University of Hawai'i Press.

Hewitt, M. (2005). *Catch wrestling: A wild and wooly look at the early days of pro wrestling in America*. Boulder, CO: Paladin Press

Hobsbawn, E. (1990). *Nations and nationalism since 1780*. Cambridge: Cambridge University Press.

Kiku, K. (2004). The development of sport in Japan: Martial arts and baseball. In Dunning, E., et al. (eds.), *Sports histories: figurational studies of the development of modern sports* (pp. 153–171). New York: Routledge.

Loy, J. & Elvogue, J. (1970). Racial segregation in American sport. *International Review of Sport Sociology* 5, 5–23.

Mandell, R. (1984). *Sport: A cultural history*. New York: Columbia University Press.

Mogull, R. (1981). Racial discrimination in professional sports. *Arena Review* 5(2): 12–15.

Mondak, J. (1989). The politics of professional wrestling. *Journal of Popular Culture* 23(2): 139–149.

Morton, G. & O'Brien, G. (1985). *Wrestling to rasslin': Ancient sport to American spectacle*. Bowling Green, OH: Bowling Green State University Popular Press.

Mrozek, D. (1983). *Sport and American mentality, 1880–1910*. Knoxville: University of Tennessee Press.

Pope, S. (1997). *Patriotic games: Sporting traditions in the American imagination, 1876–1926*. Oxford, UK: Oxford University Press.

Rainville, R. et al. (1978). Recognition of covert racial prejudice. *Journalism Quarterly* 55(2): 256–259.

Rickard, J. (1999). "The spectacle of excess": The emergence of modern professional wrestling in the United States and Australia. *Journal of Popular Culture* 33(1): 129–137.

Rosenblum, M. (1981). Martial arts poetics. *Journal of American Culture* 4(3): 148–153.

Sabo, D. (1985). Sport, patriarchy, and male identity. *Arena Review* 9(2): 1–30.

Savenga, D. (1995). The problem of wrestling 'styles' in the modern Olympic Games: A failure of Olympic philosophy. *Citius, Altius, Fortius* (now *Journal of Olympic Sport History*) 3(3): 19–29.

Schneider, J. & Eitzen, D. (1979). Racial discrimination in American sports.

Journal of Sport Behavior 2(3): 136–142.

Shun, I. (1998). The invention of the martial arts: Kano Jigoro and Kodokan judo. In S. Vlastos (ed.), *Mirror of modernity: Invented traditions of modern Japan* (pp. 163–173). Berkeley, CA: University of California Press.

Snyder, L. (1990). *Encyclopedia of nationalism*. New York: Paragon House.

Svinth, J. (2000a). Sizing 'em up: Statistical relationships between various combative sports in the Japanese American communities of the Pacific Northwest, circa 1910 to circa 1942. In *Yo: Journal of Alternate Perspectives*. Available: http://ejmas.com/jalt/jaltart_svinth1_0300.htm.

Svinth, J. (2000b). Women who would not be sheep. In *Yo: Journal of Alternate Perspectives*. Available: http://ejmas.com/jalt/jaltart_svinth4_1199.htm.

Svinth, J. (2001). The evolution of women's judo, 1900–1945. In *Yo: Journal of Alternate Perspectives*. Available: http://ejmas.com/jalt/jaltart_svinth_0201.htm.

Svinth, J. (2003). Getting a grip: Judo in the Nikkei communities of the Pacific Northwest, 1900–1950. Guelph, Ontario: *Electronic Journals of Martial Arts and Science*.

Terry, T. (1902). Jiu-jutsu, Japanese self-defense without weapons. *Outing 41*, 12–18.

Wilson, G. (Ed.)(2000). The history of Japanese immigration. *Brown Quarterly* 3(4). Available: http://brownvboard.org/brwnqurt/03-4/03-4a.htm.

Newspapers:	Referred to as:
Chicago Record-Herald	CRH
Harper's Weekly	HW
Los Angeles Times	LAT
Mind and Body	MAB
New York Times	NY
Oakland Tribune	OT
Salt Lake Herald	SLH
San Francisco Call	SFC
Seattle Times	ST

Masato Tamura, Ryoichi Iwakiri, & The Fife Judo Dojo, 1923–1942

by Joseph Svinth, M.A.

The father I thought so strict
Where did he conceal
Such tender feelings
Revealed in those gentle letters?
Many days I cried.
– Teiko Tomita (Nomura, 1987: 19)

Judo Tournament at the Fife Dojo, March 1938.
Photo from the Boland Collection,
courtesy of the Washington State
Historical Society, Tacoma, Washington.

Fife is a farm town located about two miles northeast of Tacoma, Washington. The first Japanese immigrant (*issei*) to farm the region was probably Heishiro Mihara,[1] who leased twenty acres from the Puyallup Indians Mary Charley and William McShill in 1897. Mihara then brought over his brothers-in-law Gorimatsu, Heisuke, Toichi, and Tokichi Ohashi to help him clear and work the property. Other pioneers included Soroku Kuramoto, Shintaro Mukai, and Yokichi Nakanishi (Watanabe, 1986: 86–88; Magden, 1998: 35–36).

A local landowner, John McAleer, believed that having people of different races work together would overcome racism and nationalism. By 1907, there were about thirty Issei families working McAleer properties in the area. By the mid-1910's, this number had grown to about one hundred and thirty, plus more than two hundred children. From 1910 to 1930, Japanese comprised the largest group of non-European ethnic females in Washington State (Watanabe, 1986: 86–88; Magden, 1998: 35–36; Nomura, 1987: 15).

To educate these children in Japanese culture, history, and language, sixteen issei farmers organized a Fife Language School Support Association in June 1909. The teachers were Tomehachi Nagai and his wife Yoneko (Magden, 1998: 69–70).

A schoolhouse capable of holding thirty-five students was built in late 1912. A *Seinen Kai* (Young People's Club or Association) was added in July 1915. The club's missions included cultivating lofty ideals and character in young people, teaching an appreciation for traditional Japanese values, and improving relations between Japanese and European-Americans. Members paid about a dollar per child per month. With that money, club leaders paid rent and bought books and sports equipment. While the outdoor sport of choice was baseball, indoor sports included judo and kendo. The club met every Sunday, and had about thirty members in 1917 (Magden, 1998: 69–70; Watanabe, 1986: 95–96).

Fife Yudansha (judo black belts), 1940.
Front row, left to right: Masato Tamura, Richard Hayashi,
Yasuyuki Kamagai (Seattle Dojo supervisor), Ryoichi Iwakiri.
Second row, left to right: George Iwakiri, Leo Kawasaki, Jack Ohashi,
Seiichi Yamada, Masaru Tamura, Joe Mizumoto, Hikaru Tamura,
Hiroshi Masuda, Sunji Dogen.
Photo courtesy of George & Risa Kawasaki.

Note: The SJY patch stands for "Seattle Judo Yudanshakai." It was worn by men who were part of the team that went to Los Angeles in 1939. The other patch is that of the Eatonville Dojo (Eatonville is a logging town southeast of Tacoma whose club was led by Masato Tamura. An article about this club should appear in *Columbia: The Magazine of the Washington State Historical Society*, in late 2000).

Parents soon found that American-born sons usually preferred playing sports to attending language school. So, in 1923, Fife farmers Hikozo ("Harry") Kawasaki and Kichigoro ("Kay") Yamamoto donated a barn and some mats to the Seinen Kai, and arranged for a local man to teach judo to community youths. From late September until mid-May, the Fife Dojo was open three nights a week. Like most rural judo clubs, the Fife Dojo closed during the summer. The reason was, of course, that the barn was needed for storing crops and the boys and men were busy with the harvest (Edith Kuramoto, personal communication, September 25, 1997).

Ryoichi Iwakiri was the local man who taught at the Fife club. Born in Ehime Prefecture, Japan, in 1899, Iwakiri started studying judo at the St. Paul and Tacoma lumber company's judo club around 1917. His early students included George Kawasaki, Jack Ohashi, and Masato Tamura (*Japanese-American Courier*, hereafter referred to as JAC, February 12, 1938: 4).[2]

His first dojo was far from fancy. For instance, the original mat consisted of canvas stretched from wall to wall over sawdust. The walls had no insulation, and "on cold winter nights," said the *Japanese-American Courier* many years later, "many can hark back to those times when we used to toast our toes at spots which glowed red hot on an old cracked stove" (JAC, February 12, 1938: 4). Still, it beat walking a couple miles into Tacoma two or three nights a week. "We went to school in Tacoma," recalled former Fife resident Joe Kosai in 1998, "and used to walk there and back every day. Just the other day I walked the route for the first time in years. It was a lot longer than I remembered. The hills were steeper, too" (Joe Kosai, personal communication, March 16, 1998).

Although Fife judoka surely participated in tournaments in Tacoma and Seattle from 1924 to 1927, I have seen no record of the results. Iwakiri was evidently an active tournament player. He later told his student, Jerry Dalien, that the only Seattle judoka who could beat him was Kaimon Kudo, a Seattle Dojo star who later became a well-known professional wrestler (Dalien, 1988: 23). Therefore, Fife Dojo's recorded history begins with Jack Ohashi's victory over Seattle Dojo's Michio Shinoda on November 18, 1928 (JAC, September 22, 1928: 2; JAC, November 24, 1928: 2). During another Seattle tournament held on January 18, 1931, Masato ("Mac") Tamura was the star (JAC, January 24, 1931: 2). As a result, he received promotion to first dan. His teacher, Iwakiri, simultaneously received promotion to second dan (JAC, February 20, 1931: 2; JAC, March 11, 1933: 2).

In those days, belts were white, brown, or black, and the chief promotion criterion was tournament success. Traditional throwing forms (*kata*) and meditation were taught only to boys who asked—and boys being boys, few asked (Shinji Kozu, personal communication, September 21, 1997; Hank Ogawa, personal communication, September 22, 1997). Instead, what schoolboys wanted was outward recognition. Accordingly, in February 1931, Fife Dojo members voted to award varsity-style letters to deserving members. "The qualifications," said an article in the *Japanese-American Courier*, "were to be decided upon later. Its purpose was to create more interest in the sport, and to set a goal for the younger boys to strive toward" (JAC, February 13, 1931: 2).

On September 26, 1931, nineteen-year old Masato Tamura took over day-to-day instruction at the Fife Dojo. The stated reasons for this change were that Ryoichi Iwakiri had recently started a commercial produce business, and therefore lacked the time to attend every practice (JAC, September 26, 1931: 2; *Tacoma News Tribune*, hereafter referred to as TNT, May 27, 1987: B2). However, the unstated reason was that Mrs. Iwakiri did not support Mr. Iwakiri's love of judo. Like most issei men, Iwakiri worked ten to twelve hours a day, six days a week. Add judo classes three nights a week, plus a tournament most Sundays from January to April, and Mrs. Iwakiri's disapproval becomes eminently understandable. Indeed, to keep peace, says Iwakiri's daughter Chiyo Iida (Fujiko Gardner, personal communication from Chiyo Iida, May 4, 1997):

> Judo was rarely mentioned in our house. I never heard anything about the judo tournaments from my family. My friend, Kiyoko Yamada, kept me informed about who won. It was from her I learned about Masato's brilliant participation in judo and also about my brother's accomplishments.

For the boys in the Fife club—their ages ranged from eight to twenty—Iwakiri's absence was probably something of a blessing. Tamura was an older brother rather than a father figure, and he greatly preferred tussling on the mats to lecturing. On the other hand, Iwakiri was more of a father figure. He never learned to speak English well, and when he did speak English, it was usually to stress the importance of having strong character. The following summarizes his favorite speech. The version quoted here was given in Japanese during the 1950's, and later translated into English (Dalien, 1988: 25–26).

> As an integral part of our instruction, we are taught among other things patience, courtesy, humility, and self-discipline. What passes for acceptable conduct from some athletes should not be our goal, but rather our minimum. Self-discipline and courtesy dictate that we respect the rights of others. We are not loud, ill-mannered, or boorish. We lose graciously and win with humility. We act and dress like ladies and gentlemen both on and off the mat.
> We take great pains to inform the public that judo is different from other sports. We read about it, talk about it, write about it. We tell boys' and girls' mothers and fathers that judo will make a lady or gentleman of their son or daughter, and that judo is the missing cog in a well-rounded education. In our drive to bring judo closer to the American philosophy of competition,

we must not lose sight of these basic principles which make our sport unique.

Nothing is more striking and impressive as a tournament or practice where the players are neat, reserved, and dignified, and the judging is sincere, honest, and honorable. There is the lasting impression and the principle of judo at work. Actions do speak louder than words.

Still, with the combination of lectures, good examples, and sweat, the Fife youths soon dominated local judo tournaments. At a tournament held at the Tacoma Buddhist Church on October 11, 1931, for example, Masato Tamura, Jack Ohashi, Hiroshi Tamura, George Kawasaki, and Masaomi Kibe all won pennants (JAC, October 10, 1931: 2; JAC, October 17, 1931: 2).

While instruction was always in English at the dojo, the names of techniques were taught in Japanese. Upon entering or leaving the mat, students were expected to bow toward the instructors. Students also were expected to sit quietly when not practicing, avoid horseplay, and keep unnecessary talking to a minimum (Kenji Yaguchi, personal communication, October 3, 1997).

Fife Dojo March 5, 1934. Front row, seated left to right: Kiyoshi Kuramoto, Mitsuru Tamura, Bob Watanabe, Harry Morisaki, Leo Kawasaki, Hiro Yaguchi, unidentified, unidentified, Don Kawasaki. Second row, seated, left to right: Atsushi Kuramoto, unidentified, unidentified, Sam Uchida, Masato Tamura, Ryoichi Iwakiri, Jack Ohash, Sakahara, Seiichi Yamada, unidentified, S. Teranishi. Third row, kneeling left to right: Jin (?) Sagami, Masaru Tamura, Kimio Watanabe, Joe Mizumoto, unidentified. Fourth row, standing, left to right: Sunji Dogen, P. Tamura, George Kawasaki, Masachi Kibe. Photo courtesy of George and Risa Kawasaki.

Note: The photo on the back wall shows judo founder Kano Jigoro in his court uniform. The significance of the shield is not known. Note the canvas mats. The knotty lumber used in the construction of the barn suggests that it was built from scrap from the St. Paul and Tacoma lumber mill, which was then the world's largest.

As money was always tight, in October 1931, the Fife Seinen Kai decided that it would raise money by holding Japanese movie nights. Excepting the refreshments sold by the local Girls' Club (*Fuyo Kai*) during these movie nights, Fife youth were not exposed to club fund-raising activities. Instead, finances were handled entirely by adults. Parents whose children didn't do judo complained that judo diverted money from other youth activities. So, in January 1935 the Fife Seinen Kai and the Fife Dojo split into separate organizations (Kenji Yaguchi, personal communication, October 3, 1997; JAC, October 17, 1931: 2; JAC, January 26, 1935: 3).

The Fife Dojo hosted a tournament inside the Fife High School auditorium during the weekend of February 28 thru March 1, 1931.[3] Fife hosted another tournament at Fife High School on February 27–28, 1932. The highlight of this tournament involved Ito, a fifth-dan from a ship visiting Tacoma, throwing six local judoka during a handicap match. In competition, Masato Tamura also threw five men to take first place in his division. The *Japanese-American Courier* noted, "In promoting and making a success of the big tournament, the local mothers' group, Girls' Club and the men cooperated in every way" (JAC, March 5, 1932: 2).

So that people could work on their farms, the dojo normally closed between May and September. However, when judo's founder Kano Jigoro announced that he was going to visit Pacific Northwest Japanese language schools in late August 1932, the Fife Dojo resumed training on August second that year (JAC, August 6, 1932: 2). The extra effort paid off, too, as during the welcoming tournament held in Seattle, Jack Ohashi earned a promotion to first dan awarded by Professor Kano himself (JAC, October 15, 1932: 2).

Oral tradition has it that Professor Kano visited the Fife Dojo during the 1932 Northwest US visit. Although I have seen no photos or newspaper articles to prove either the visit or the timing, I suspect that it did take place, on August 18, 1932. Kano had a documented speaking engagement at the Tacoma Japanese Language School that evening, and while en route he probably visited the dojos in Kent, Auburn, and Fife.

In 1933, the club resumed training at its normal time, late September. In early November, Ryoichi Iwakiri loaded the boys in his truck and took them to a small tournament on Bainbridge Island. George Kawasaki returned to Fife with the first place trophy (JAC, September 29, 1933, p. 2; JAC, November 11, 1933, p. 2).

Fife was always a popular stop on the local tournament circuit. The reason was that the school auditorium held two mats rather than one, as was typical elsewhere. Therefore meets ended somewhat earlier in the evening (JAC, February 18, 1933: 2). As elsewhere, speeches, announcements, and the award of service trophies usually prefaced the bouts. For example, on March 17, 1934, Kichigoro Yamamoto and Ryoichi Iwakiri both received silver cups in appreciation of their support throughout the years. Then, to the local crowd's delight, Masato Tamura, Hikaru ("Polka") Tamura, and Joe Yamamoto went out and won medals in their respective divisions (JAC, March 17, 1934: 2).

Kichigoro ("Kay") Yamamoto, future patron of the Fife Dojo, after winning the Northwest AAU wrestling championship at 125 pounds in 1912.
Photo courtesy of Edith Yamamoto Kuramoto.

The 1935 season was among Fife's best. George Kawasaki received an honorable mention at a February 10, 1935 tournament at the Seattle Dojo (JAC, February 16, 1935: 3). Daizo ("Dykes") Itami of Fife, a former Cleveland High School four-sport letterman, took his turn by winning first place during a Tentoku Kan tournament held March 3, 1935 (JAC, March 9, 1935: 3). Finally, Masato Tamura won an upset victory over Seattle Dojo's Kaimon Kudo at South Park on March 10, 1935, and came home with second place (JAC, March 16, 1935: 3; *Great Northern Daily News*, hereafter referred to as GND, March 11, 1935: 8).

In 1936, a small child playing with matches started a fire that razed the Fife Dojo (Edith Kuramoto, personal communication, September 25, 1997). Since Japanese-American boys provided the backbone of the Fife High School football, wrestling, and track teams, the judo club had no trouble arranging temporary sanctuary at Fife Junior High School. The Tacoma Dojo also welcomed Fife judoka. However, living on charity wasn't the same as having a dojo, and the Fife community responded to the disaster by building a judo wing to the Fife Japanese Language School (Edith Kuramoto, personal communication, September 25, 1997).

Other than the loss of its dojo, 1936 was another good year for the Fife Dojo. In March 1936, Masato Tamura, second dan, threw Kuniyuki Kaname, third dan, of Tentoku Kan in a well-publicized match.[4] In October 1936, a twenty-three-man Northwest all-star judo team that included Masato Tamura, Jack Ohashi, and George Kawasaki went to Los Angeles for a tournament with a California all-star team. Said the *Great Northern Daily News* afterward (October 27, 1936: 8):

> Wins were scarce [for the Northwest team] until Masato Tamura, who ranked fifth on the Seattle team, turned the tables and hurled three men to the mat. He drew with Warren Lewis, Negro judoist.[5]

Hank Ogawa and Hiroshi Tamura resting during the training preceding the 1939 all-star tournament in Los Angeles. *Photo courtesy of Hank Ogawa.*

As a result of this outstanding performance, Professor Kano personally promoted Tamura to third dan in California (JAC, October 31, 1936: 3). Although this meant that Tamura was now technically senior to Iwakiri, the rank inversion did not affect their friendship. Says Iwakiri's daughter, Chiyo Iida, "My father was very proud to have the Tamura family participating in the Fife judo. Of course, Masato was the number one judoist in the region, as well as other regions. The other brothers did very well too" (Fujiko Gardner, personal communication from Chiyo Iida, May 4, 1997; Fujiko Gardner, personal communication, July 12, 1997). Tamura was equally proud of his teacher, and after the war, whenever visiting his family in Tacoma, he would visit Iwakiri at his house. Adds Stewart Bush, one of Iwakiri's postwar seniors, "And Mr. Iwakiri didn't let anybody inside his house!" (Stewart Bush, personal communication, August 30, 1997; Fujiko Gardner, personal communication, October 28, 1997).

Besides doing judo, Fife nisei (people born in America of issei parents) were also active in the Fife High School wrestling team, where they dominated the lower weights. With the exception of heavyweight Joe Yamamoto, Swiss-Americans dominated the upper weights (Leslie Sandvig, personal communication, August 14, 1997). Prewar all-Northwest wrestling champions from Fife High School included Don Kawasaki, Leo Kawasaki, and Kenji Yaguchi. George Makoto Iwakiri was also active in both wrestling and judo.[6]

Les Sandvig was the wrestling coach at Fife. Due to federal salary subsidies, Sandvig earned $150 a month while his principal earned just $90. To be sure,

Sandvig earned all that extra money, the principal assigned him every extra duty he could find, including wrestling coach. (Few Northwest high schools of the 1930's had wrestling teams.) As Sandvig later recalled:

> The teachers did a lot of after school hours of work—with school programs, P.T.A. meetings, etc. There was no such thing as overtime!
> The wrestling coach job was enjoyable—working with the kids. Joe Yamamoto at 165 pounds, had no partner to work out with, so he and I spent a lot of time working out (my weight at that time was 170, 175). The things he taught me—together we made a great team, and he made a better coach of me.
> Often there would be judo exhibition matches to raise money for the athletic departments. The Japanese who had graduated from Fife and lived in the community were available for these events. Masato Tamura and Sunji Dogen were glad to support this effort.
> – (Sandvig, personal communication, August 14, 1997)

On January 31, 1937, the Fife and Tacoma clubs held a joint tournament at the Tacoma Buddhist Church. This was in preparation for a rematch with the Californians to be held in Seattle over the weekend of April 3–4, 1937. In the individual competition, Hikaru Tamura lost to California's Hikaru Nakao and Masato Tamura drew with California's Mitsuo Kimura. In the team competition, Hikaru Tamura drew with California's Oseko and Jack Ohashi drew with California's Asano (JAC, April 10, 1937: 3).[7]

On February 7, 1938, Fife Dojo celebrated the opening of its new judo hall. The master of ceremonies was Tsugio Yaguchi, and speakers included the head of Kodokan judo in the Northwest, Yasuyuki Kumagai of Seattle. The *Japanese-American Courier* described the new facility, which was attached to the Japanese Language School, as "well-lighted, well-heated, and the mat consists of rubber-cushioned imported tatami—a veritable judoist's paradise" (February 12, 1938: 4).

On March 20, 1938, Fife celebrated the opening with a tournament. Spectators included Tacoma photographer Marvin Boland, who hoped to get some action photos for *Life* magazine,[8] and officers from the Pierce County Sheriff's Department and the Washington State Patrol (*North American Times*, hereafter referred to as NAT, March 17, 1938: 1).

Judo founder Kano Jigoro visited the Northwest for the last time in April 1938. During this visit, Kano promoted Iwakiri to third dan and his fourteen-year old son George Makoto Iwakiri to first dan. While Dennis Helm has claimed these as Kano's last promotions, that is probably not the case. For one thing, other Northwest judoka, including Ei'ichi Koiwai of Seattle, received promotion the same night. It seems petty to argue about who stood last in line. More importantly, Kano visited Vancouver, British Columbia, on April 21–22, 1938, and probably promoted someone there before leaving (Dalien, 1988: 13–14; Ei'ichi Koiwai, personal communication, July 12, 1997).

The certificates that Kano left behind also caused some confusion. Kano had signed them using the phrase "*kiichi sai,*" which means, "return to the original way." In 1977, Dennis Helm speculated that Kano meant that the Northwest judoka, many of whom were Christian, should take up Zen Buddhism (Helm, 1977: 16). Of course, Kano meant no such thing. Kiichi Sai was simply a pen name he adopted upon turning seventy. Therefore, when he visited Seattle in 1938, he unsurprisingly signed promotion certificates, "Kano Kiichi Sai" (Dalien, 1988: 14; Nakayama, 1984: 201).

Fife hosted another regional tournament on February 12, 1939. The purpose of this tournament was to decide who would represent the Northwest during an upcoming tournament in California. Seven of the thirty players sent to Los Angeles came from Fife. These were Masato Tamura, Hikaru Tamura, Hiroshi Tamura, Jack Ohashi, Sunji Dogen, George Kawasaki, and Joe Yamamoto. The Northwest team trained hard, and while they lost the individual matches 7–11 on March 4, 1939, its members evened things up the following day by winning the team competition (JAC, February 25, 1939, p. 3; NAT, March 6, 1939, p. 1).

As many of these young Northwesterners had never been south of Portland, Oregon, the two days spent visiting San Francisco's Golden Gate International Exposition on the way back from Los Angeles were the true highlight of the trip. Auburn judoka Toshio Yamanaka recalled:

> The Japanese Pavilion and Hawaii Exposition were the team's favorite places to meet and get together. That's because the many girls working at the two places were nisei students at U.C. Berkeley and were there helping and working to help pay their college expenses. They were very friendly and treated us extra good so our car drivers drove them to their homes when it came time for them to get off work. The rest of us had to wait over an hour longer than the time set to leave to get a ride back to our hotel. Most of us in those days were rather girl shy, but the girls were all pretty and very nice and friendly and treated us like we were a special group. So we weren't upset to wait for the guys to take them home. But when we got back [Yasuyuki] Kumagai Sensei had us all stand in the main hotel lobby and gave us a lecture to never do such a thing again, to make all of us wait. It was the first and only lecture that we got from our sensei. This world's fair was really the greatest.
> – (Yamanaka personal communications, February 3, 19, & March 11, 1998)

Being otherwise responsible young men, the travelers bought souvenirs for their stay-at-home friends. Recalled Ryoichi Iwakiri's daughter, Chiyo Iida (Fujiko Gardner, personal communication from Chiyo Iida, May 4, 1997):

> I have a good memory about our [family's] relation with them [Hiroshi and Hikaru Tamura, both of whom were years older than she]. In 1939 they went to the World's Fair in San Francisco (Treasure Island) and brought us a lot of mementos from the Fair. I was so proud I wore my bracelet to school and everyone was so envious.

In January 1941, Masato Tamura's sister, Tadako,[9] saw an advertisement announcing a full-time job teaching judo at Chicago's Jiu-Jitsu Institute (GND, January 15, 1941: 8). She mentioned this to her brother, who immediately applied. He got the job and left for the "Windy City" in March 1941 (GND, February 28, 1941: 8; JAC, March 1, 1941: 3). Besides being lauded in the local papers, Tamura received various honors at local tournaments plus a send-off banquet from the Fife Dojo (GND, September 24, 1940: 8; NAT, November 17, 1938: 1). The latter likely took place at Fife's Poodle Dog Cafè on a Friday night in late February. The main course was probably chicken, with the men drinking beer and the youths drinking apple cider. And afterwards there were likely speeches culminating in a stirring rendition of "Auld Lange Syne" (NAT, 1940, September 30: 1).

During World War II, Fife's Japanese-Americans were relocated to concentration camps in California and Idaho. Because he lived in Chicago, Masato Tamura avoided being relocated. Hiroshi, who had been drafted in 1940, also avoided relocation. However, the rest of the Tamura family was sent to Minidoka Relocation Center in Hunt, Idaho.

During the summer of 1943, Masato Tamura received permission to visit his family at Minidoka. There he found his brothers active in the camp judo club, and even arranged for his mother to stitch judo jackets for his Chicago judo students (Fujiko Gardner, personal communication, June 8, 1997). Mrs. Tamura always was an enthusiastic supporter of her sons' judo practice (Fujiko Gardner, personal communication, March 16, 1998). Soon after, both Masaru and Mitsuru Tamura enlisted in the US Army and served in the 442nd Regimental Combat Team. Masaru was killed in Italy in April 1945.

After the war, most of the surviving Tamura boys stayed in the Midwest. Ryoichi Iwakiri returned to Fife in 1947. While his first postwar judo dojo was a friend's garage, around 1952 he moved it inside the old Tacoma Japanese Language School. His dojo was in the basement. The floor area measured about 20' x 20', and the tatami were provided by friends (NT, August 16, 1952: 2; Washington 1995).

Ryoichi Iwakiri, mid-1960's. Photo courtesy of Hank Ogawa.

Although Iwakiri retired from active training around 1957, he remained affiliated with the Tacoma-Fife Dojo until his death in May 1987. Most of what he taught during the last thirty years of his life was philosophy. Favorite sayings included, "Success is like your eyebrows. It's in front of you all the time, you just can't see it," and "Victory even before the battle is for the person who is embraced with compassion and no thought of himself" (Stewart Bush, personal communication, March 10, 1998).

A prospective student once asked Iwakiri what it took to become a judo master. Three things, he replied: the first two were practice, and the third was more practice. "That's not what I meant," said the student; "what is the key to mastering the long run?" Replied Iwakiri, "In the long run, we are all dead." Another student asked what he would be taught. To which Iwakiri replied, "I can't teach you very much, but you can learn a lot" (Stewart Bush, personal communication, November 28, 1997). And, shortly before his death, Iwakiri told his longtime student Jerry Dalien:

> [Kano Jigoro] told me once that I must be strong in mind and body always, and help others in life. I appreciate all you peoples who come and see me. I am old now and peoples have no time for them. Mr. Yamashita, Mr. Bush, Mr. Demorest, and you Mr. Dalien are fine students of Kano's judo.[10] Mr. Uchida, he is important mans in judo—you tell him good-bye for me. I am not important persons, I have done nothing great, I have no schooling. You please make any honor for me, just judo. Okay? I do not have long time left to live anymore, but want you to keep my judo, please? Okay?
> – (Dalien, 1988: 23–24)

Vince Tamura, three time U.S. AAU judo champion,
training at his dojo in Dallas, Texas, in 1997.
Photo courtesy of Fujiko Tamura Gardner.

**Judo tournament at
the Fife Dojo, March 1938.**
Photo from the Boland Collection,
courtesy of the Washington State
Historical Society, Tacoma, Washington.

Following the war, Masato Tamura also remained active in judo. In 1944, he bought the Jiu-Jitsu Institute of America from Harry Auspitz. In 1949, he was elected president of the Chicago Judo Black Belt Association, and in 1958 he became president of the US Judo Federation. Yet he was not just another judo politician, for as late as 1964 he was still winning US masters championships.[11] More importantly, he remained a friend and mentor to his many students. As one of them wrote following Tamura's death on June 10, 1982, "With modesty and humility he characterized the true judo spirit" ("Masato Tamura, Hachidan," in Masato Tamura collection).

Other former Fife judoka also remained with judo until age or infirmity forced their retirement. For example, Vince Tamura moved to Chicago in June 1945. After completing high school and military service in Korea, he went on to become a three-time AAU national judo champion. In August 1960, he relocated to Dallas, where he was still teaching judo in 1998. After separation from the service, Mitsuru Tamura also moved to Chicago, where he was an instructor at his brother's Jiu-Jitsu Institute for many years. Hikaru Tamura taught judo in Ogden, Utah. Hiroshi Tamura taught judo in Chicago and France. George Iwakiri, George Kawasaki, and Leo Kawasaki taught judo at the Tacoma-Fife Dojo. Finally, Kenji Yaguchi taught judo in Ontario, Oregon, and was chairman of the Oregon AAU Judo Committee from 1958 to 1966 (Stewart Bush, personal communication, November 28, 1997; Kenji Yaguchi, personal communication, June 22, 1997).[12]

And so the falls first learned in Mr. Yamamoto's barn in the 1920's continue to echo throughout North American judo.

Endnotes

[1] Although Japanese put family names before personal names, most of the people named in this paper were or eventually became US citizens. Therefore, it better reflects the way they described themselves if their names are written personal name, family name rather than the other way around. To keep things simple, the occasional Japanese names are also written in the American fashion.

[2] The history of the Fife Dojo—given in Helm (July 1977) and reprinted almost verbatim (albeit without any attribution to Helm's editorial team or acknowledgment of US Judo Federation copyright) by Corcoran and Farkas (1988: 212-214, 217)—is wrong in almost every detail. On the other hand, the history given in Helm, Armetta, and Wickham (May 1973: 14-15) is generally accurate except for spellings.

[3] Photograph (cir. 1931-3) of a Fife High School tournament in the Joseph Svinth collection

[4] Published articles and photographs owned by Mr. Tamura's widow, Rose Tamura.

[5] Reasonable numbers of early twentieth-century judoka were not of Japanese ancestry. In California, for example, non-Japanese judoka included San Jose State's Emilio Bruno, Los Angeles' Jack Sergel and Warren Lewis, and Stockton's Robert E. West. In British Columbia, there were a number of Royal Canadian Mounted Police judoka, and in Washington State, there was Stanley McDonald in Seattle and Vernon Anderson in Winslow. There were of course more non-Japanese jujutsu teachers and students elsewhere, especially in New York City and the upper Midwest. While most teachers and students were male, there were female students in New York City and Los Angeles, plus at least

one female instructor in Wisconsin.
6. See Fife High School's *Trojan, 1935–1942*. Fife nisei did equally well in postwar AAU wrestling. For example, Hisashi Watanabe lettered in wrestling at Fife in 1946 and 1947, and qualified for the US AAU Nationals in Ames, Iowa, in 1948 (*Northwest Times*, hereafter referred to as NWT, May 1, 1948: 3).
7. See the Keigi Horiuchi collection. The first names for the California judoka were not noted in the reporting.
8. While Boland's records at the Washington State Historical Society in Tacoma date the surviving photographs to March 30, 1938, that was probably the day he developed them, as the tournament took place a week earlier. Unfortunately, the pictures were too blurred to make *Life* magazine.
9. Tadako Tamura is an excellent writer, and examples of her essays appeared in the *North American Times* on January 4, 1938 and May 14, 1938, and the *Great Northern Daily News* on January 1, 1940. Her postwar pen name was Thea Mori. For a brilliant example of her mature style, see "Salmon Creek This Week" in the *White Center News*, May 26, 1960.
10. Stewart Bush, Robert Demorest, and Jerry Dalien were among Iwakiri's postwar seniors. Masao Yamashita was a prewar friend from Auburn who later established the Boise Valley Judo Club in Caldwell, Idaho. George Uchida was a former San Jose State University judo coach who took a job teaching judo in the Kent-Meridian High School program after one day realizing that the spirit of judo was not found in winning medals, but in working with kids.
11. Tamura became known nationwide through television. The most famous television appearances included his daughter Diane. The act was usually nothing more than Tamura doing a few throws and falls with his daughter, and then talking about judo. The first took place on Chicago television on February 10, 1952. The popularity of their act lead to national television exposure beginning in June 1952. For contemporary accounts of Tamura's postwar career, see NT, November 3, 1948: 1; NT, August 20, 1949: 4; NT, August 31, 1949: 3; NT, February 16, 1952: 4; NT, June 18, 1952: 4.
12. "Members of the Tamura Family Involved with Tacoma-Fife Dojo," unpublished typewritten document in the Fujiko Gardner collection.

Bibliography

Corcoran, J. & Farkas, E. (1988). *Martial arts: Traditions, history, people*. New York: W. H. Smith.

Dalien, J. (1988). *Judo: The life, the way, the concept*. Spanaway, WA: Self-published.

Helm, D. (Ed.). (1977, July) The history of American judo. *Judo USA*, 3(3): 16–17.

Helm, D., Armetta, P. & Wickham, D. (1973, May). The Pacific North West 1907 to 1941. *Judo Illustrated*, 7(1): 14–15.

Magden, R. (1998). *Furusato: Tacoma-Pierce County Japanese*. Tacoma, WA: Tacoma Japanese Community Service: 35–36.

"Masato Tamura, Hachidan," unpublished document in Masato Tamura collection.
"Members of the Tamura Family Involved with Tacoma-Fife Dojo," unpublished typewritten document in Fujiko Gardner collection.
Mori, T. (1960, May 26). Salmon Creek this week. *White Center News*.
Nakayama, G. (1984). *Issei: Stories of Japanese Canadian pioneers*. Toronto: NC Press.
Nomura, G. (1987). Tsugiki, a grafting a history of a Japanese pioneer woman in Washington State. *Women's Studies*, 14(1): 19.
Trojan, 1935–1942. (n.d.). Fife, Washington: Fife High School.
Washington State Judo 1995 Hall of Fame (n.d.). No city or publisher given.
Watanabe, J. (Trans.) (1986). *History of the Japanese of Tacoma*. Seattle: Pacific Northwest Council, Japanese American Citizens League.

Newspapers

Great Northern Daily News (referred to as GND).

Japanese-American Courier (referred to as JAC).

North American Times (referred to as NAT).

Northwest Times (referred to as NWT).

Tacoma News Tribune (referred to as TNT).

The School of Hard Knocks: Seattle's Kurosaka/Tentoku Kan Dojo 1928-1942

by Joeseph Svinth, M.A.

Winter seclusion
Kotatsu* reverie
Faces of childhood.
– Richard Hayes

* *Low table with heater beneath*

At 8 p.m. on Sunday, 11 November 1928—the coronation date of the Japanese Emperor Hirohito—the Kurosaka Dojo opened at 900 Yesler Way in Seattle. Its name was that of its chief instructor, Kurosaka Hiroshi, 3rd-dan. Permission to open the school had been granted by Nagaoka Hidekazu, 8th-dan chief instructor at the Tokyo Normal School, and stylistic leader of the Hojin Dai Nippon Butokukai, a Kyoto martial art association whose politics were often at odds with those of the Tokyo-based Kodokan.[1]

Kurosaka believed that judo was the best kind of exercise, both physically and mentally, for young people. Americans who wished to learn the art were welcome in his club, he said, as this would give them a better understanding of Japanese people. Nevertheless, all of his approximately twenty students were nisei.[2]

From the mid-1920s until November 1928, Kurosaka had been chief instructor at the Seattle Dojo. His split with the Seattle Dojo came over a number of small grievances. Money probably played a role. The Seattle Dojo was trying to raise money to build a new dojo on Washington Street (it was then located in the basement of the Tacoma Hotel), and Kurosaka apparently disagreed with the way the money was being allocated. Additionally, there were the usual dojo politics. Kurosaka was a Butokukai man, and the Seattle Dojo was a Kodokan school. As noted above, the Butokukai and the Kodokan were rivals even in Japan, and apparently their rivalry carried over to Seattle. Finally, there seem to have been personality conflicts between Kurosaka and the Seattle Dojo's leadership.[3]

The split between Kurosaka and the Seattle Dojo was acrimonious. The boys in one club would call the boys from the other club *yogore* ("dirty guys"), and claimed that what they did wasn't real judo. Of course this was not true. While Butokukai schools may have placed more emphasis on ground wrestling than Kodokan schools, their technical standards were virtually identical. Meanwhile, the boys' parents muttered calumnies against the leaders of the other school, and said that their teachers did things which did not set good examples for children.

Once again, this wasn't true. Nevertheless, such bitterness led to significant disharmony in Seattle judo. Matters improved over time, but it wasn't until June 1938 that the *North American Times* could say:[5]

> Tentokukwan Dojo and Seattle Dojo were at forks' end with each other for several years. Rivalry approached the fight stage, as each fought to gain more new members to increase its own prestige.
>
> Now, however, things are different. There is, of course, rivalry between the local groups, but it is of the friendly, competitive kind. The coming of the present judo instructors, Sakata and Kumagai, as well as the formation of the all-star black belt team to tour California, were no doubt factors which brought about the more peaceable era in the judo front.

Young judoka pictured with Kano Jigoro. Professor Kano sits in the middle, while Seattle's Uzo Shiji stands at the far left. The others are unidentified. Photo courtesy of Kuqo Shinji.

Kurosaka Dojo made its first important tournament appearance in Vancouver, British Columbia, on Sunday, 9 February 1930. With only about twenty members, mostly teenaged or younger, it was hard for the Kurosaka Dojo to make much of a dent on bigger clubs with older, more experienced members. However, Kurosaka was a first-rate coach, and his young men tried.[6] Tad Kuniyuki, one of those original students, later recalled:[7]

> Mr. Kurosaka was the best judo instructor for the young students because he taught each of the students the name of the *waza* [technique] and why the waza worked when applied properly (the laws of physics) and also how to counter it. He also started the use of colored belts for the young teenagers and younger so they would have a higher belt to work for before getting a brown belt.

THE SEATTLE DOJO group photo circa 1929 at its "old location" under the Tacoma Hotel shortly before Mr. Kurosaka split away from Kurosaka Dojo. Photo courtsy of Kozu Shinji. **First row, kneeling, L to R:** Sam Kozu, Ben Terao, Tom Kubota, Abe Mitsuji, Kozu Shinji, Tom Mayeda, Asakura Yukio, Terumasa "Pan" Furuta, Elmer Tazuma, Taka "Tom" Okazaki, Ihashi Mamoru, Kubo Kazuo, Iseki Tsutomu, unidentified, George Ogishima, Furuta Yoshio, Henry Uyehara, unidentified, unidentified, Kimura Michio, Frank Yoshitake, George Hasegawa; **Second row, seated, L to R:** unidentified, Sakano Ichiro (1st-kyu), Kanda Yoshiharu (1st-kyu), Masachi "George" Maniwa, (1st-kyu), Suzuki Eitaro (3rd-dan), Kurosaka Hiroshi (3rd-dan), Masataro "John" Shibata (2nd-dan), Hama Hideo (2nd-dan), Mochizuki Goro (1st-kyu), Kudo Kaimon, 1st-kyu); **Third row, standing, L to R:** unidentified, Kaname "Ken" Kuniyuki, unidentified, Yoshijima Takeo (?), unidentified, Hamamoto Kiichi, unidentified, Bill Yorozu, unidentified, unidentified, Kubota Takeshi; **Fourth row, standing, L to R:** unidentified, Nitta Susuma, Sakuma Takeo, Hideo "Lindy" Uyehara, Horiuchi Takeo, Tad Kuniyuki, Iwana Shiro, Iwana Saburo, Sam Asanuma, Yorita Tatsuo, Nakagawa Nobushi, unidentified. Identification courtesy of Tad Kuniyuki.

Sometime during the spring of 1930, Kurosaka discovered he had tuberculosis. He went to Los Angeles to see doctors, which caused the newspaper to prematurely report that he died there of the disease. Yet, while his condition was fatal, and would soon cause his death,[8] Kurosaka did not quit judo until the very end. Said the *Japanese American Courier*, "Kurosaka had an easy time taking the 'yodan' or fourth grade title by defeating eightmen in about seven minutes" during a tournament at the Nippon Kan Theater on 18 January 1931.[9] In April 1931, he also gave what seems to have been his final public demonstration to the members of the posh 7 Washington Athletic Club in Seattle."

In February 1931, the Kurosaka Dojo opened a satellite dojo at the Seinen Kai (Youth Club) Hall of the Nichiren Buddhist temple. The reason was to get better facilities. "When Tentokukan was on Yesler Way," says Koiwai Eichi, "we had a dressing room but no showers. In the back of the dojo were hard straw tatamis while in front was a softer canvas mat which of course we practiced on whenever we could."[11] In 1934, Kurosaka Dojo vacated the premises on Yesler altogether, and with the move into the Seinen Kai facilities changed its name to Tentoku Kan.[12] Although I haven't found anyone who remembers what the name means—most Seattle nisei spoke little Japanese and read less—it probably means "Heavenly Virtue Hall."[13]

In October 1931, Torigoye Kanezo became Tentoku Kan's first junior star. He accomplished this by winning the junior division of a tournament held at the Tacoma Buddhist Temple. Four months later, in February 1932, Seattle judoka celebrated twenty five years of Kodokan judo in the northwest by holding a huge tournament at the Nippon Kan Theater in Seattle.[14]

This was a single-elimination tourney, starting with the juniors. Red and White Contests (*kohaku shobu*) were included. White Team was Seattle Dojo, South Park, and White River Dojo. The Red Team was Kent, Tentoku Kan, Tacoma, and Fife. In *Fighting Spirit of Japan* (1982), E.J. Harrison described Red and White competitions as follows:[15]

> The competitors are divided into two teams (red and white), each team having its leader and being arranged according to the degree of skill possessed by the members. Thus the contest will begin with the least proficient and youngest opponents of the lower grades, and each bout is decided by the first fall or point scored instead of the best two out of three. . . . Ultimately the two best men on either side meet and fight it out. . . . At such moments, not unnaturally, intense excitement prevails.

Below: Aerial view of the Kodokan 1935. Photo courtesy of Koqu Shinji.

In other words, everyone screamed and shouted. However, during individual competition, strict silence was maintained in the auditorium, much to the surprise of European-American observers.

It was during such a Red and White contest in Fife in February 1932 that Kuniyuki Kaname became Tentoku Kan's second nisei star. For, on the strength of the twenty-two-year-old former football star's victory, Tentoku Kan won its first ever senior division pennant.[16]

In October 1932, Yorita Tatsuo, who had just been promoted to 1st-dan, sailed to Japan.[17] In Tokyo, he trained under Professor Iizuka Kunisaburo, 8th-dan (later 10th-dan), a man E.J. Harrison once described as "a miniature Hercules in physique and possessed of astonishing skill and agility."[18] In April 1933, Yorita was promoted to 2nd-dan, making him the first Seattle nisei to receive that rank in Japan.[19] Kuniyuki Kaname followed Yorita to Japan in October 1934. There he too studied with Professor Iizuka.[20] However, while going to Japan was good for Kuniyuki and Yorita, their departure left just five black belts at the Tentoku Kan, none of whom were highly ranked. These were Sakano Ichiro, supervisor, 2nd-dan; Hama Hideo, 2nd-dan; Nitta Susumu, 1st-dan; Horiuchi Takeo, 1st-dan; and Torigoye Kanezo, 1st-dan. Reflecting the changing demographics of the times, the first two men were *issei*, while the latter were *nisei*.

Undaunted, the Tentoku Kan men persevered, and even hosted their own regional tournament at the Nippon Kan Theater on Sunday, 29 January 1933. Explained Sakano to a *Japanese American Courier* reporter: "It is understood the meet will be made into a competitive tournament in which every participant will be forced to give his utmost from the start to the finish."[21]

The Kodokan (1935) at street level. Notice the scarcity of automobiles and the absence of neon. Photo courtesy of Kozu Shinji.

Although White River Dojo, a Seattle Dojo affiliate, won that particular tournament, Tentoku Kan's never-say-die attitude was soon rewarded. At a judo tournament held at the Nippon Kan Theater on Saturday, 3 March 1934, Nitta Susumu, who was still three weeks away from his fifteenth birthday, took first in men's black belt competition. At a Seattle Dojo tournament held 10 February

1935, Nitta took second in the senior division while Frank Yoshitake took first in the junior division. A week later, however, the best any Tentoku Kan player did during their own tournament was a second place, taken by Frank Takeshita of Kent. Evidently beating the host school in its own tournament was the chief attraction of intraclub competition.[22]

About the same time (early 1934), Kiyoshi "Kelly" Uno went to Japan to study judo. Despite an appendectomy in May 1934, Uno earned his 1st dan in November by throwing one brown belt and three 1st-dans in a row, then tying a fourth. Six months later, he was promoted to 2nd-dan.[23] Kozu Shinji of the Seattle Dojo was in Japan about the same time. As Kozu recalled his year at the Kodokan:[24]

> The dojo was open every day. Since Kodokan was the headquarters, there were many hundreds of black belts training daily. All one had to do was go up to a judoist and ask to practice. Every month there was a tournament for the first four judo ranks. Depending on the record of the individual over a space of time, he was promoted to the next rank. That was how I attained the ni-dan [2nd-dan] belt rank.

Technically, added Kozu:[25]

> Judo training was much harder at Kodokan than in Seattle. In Seattle there usually was one or two yo-dan [4th-dan] and go-dan [5th-dan] judoists. At Kodokan on any day there were many high ranked judoists present throughout the day. There was no formalized sessions that I know of and so one got out of training only how much effort one put in.

Still, concluded Kozu, high school football training was often more physically demanding than judo training, and much more likely to cause debilitating injuries.[26]

Elmer Tazuma, a Tentoku Kan judoka who went to Japan on 9 September 1934, had similar experiences, saying: "I participated in judo at the high school and also visited a dojo in Kure, Japan, where I stayed with my uncle. Since I never planned to be an instructor, I only learned the fundamentals and was never outstanding like some of the students who I thought were really great."[27]

While many nisei made this trip to Japan, most did not find it an entirely pleasurable experience. Many did not speak Japanese well, and when they spoke English, they were ridiculed for their accents and their pretensions.[28] Further, flush toilets were rare, houses rarely had central heating, and the newsreels blared little but news of Japanese victories in China. Fortunately, the music was familiar. Said University of Washington graduate Kobayashi Shin in a letter home in 1937:[29]

> When I took a bath in the public bath the other day (since we have no bath in this house), the woman attendant (yes, a woman attendant in the men's section of the bath) turned on 'Singing in the Rain' and some Bing Crosby numbers. The radios have symphonies and recorded programs in the best American fashion.

Meanwhile, back in Seattle, Tentoku Kan celebrated its seventh anniversary with a tournament at the Nippon Kan on 3 March 1935. Over two hundred judoka from nine schools attended. The Tentoku Kan team, composed of Frank Yoshitake, Kato Hiroshi, and Nitta Susumu, defeated a Kent team to win the senior team trophy. Tentoku Kan juniors took second place. A scheduled and highly anticipated rematch between Kudo Kaimon and Nitta Susumu failed to happen, however, when Nitta injured his leg earlier in the evening.[30]

During a tournament at South Park on 10 March 1935, Kato Hiroshi of Tentoku Kan threw three opponents and tied a fourth to win individual honors in the team competition. This was quite an honor, as Tamura Masato of Fife led the second place finishers.[31]

A few weeks after this tournament, Nitta Susumu, Kato Hiroshi, and Shibuya Masanori traveled to Portland, Oregon, to attend Obukan Dojo's annual tournament. About the same time, Tentoku Kan's Frank Yoshitake, a star athlete in baseball, basketball, and judo, also left for Japan. Before he left, however, a special intradojo meet was held in which Yoshitake distinguished himself by throwing five opponents.[32]

On Thursday, 9 May 1935, Nitta Susumu and Kato Hiroshi gave a judo demonstration at the posh Washington Athletic Club in Seattle. They were featured on a card including boxing, wrestling, and fencing matches that was intended to raise money for the Sea Scouts. Five days later, a thirty-one-year-old Japanese businessman named Sakata Chuji arrived in Seattle.[33] Ranked 5th-dan in judo, Sakata quickly assumed the role of chief instructor at Tentoku Kan. To honor his arrival, over one hundred judoka and their friends greeted him with a banquet at the Kin Ka Low restaurant.[34]

Sakata's first official actions included awarding some well-deserved promotions. For example, on 7 June 1935, he promoted Nitta Susumu to 2nd-dan and Kato Hiroshi and Nitta Masaru to 1st-dan. Nitta Susumu was also recognized for having thrown Kudo Kaimon during a Seattle Dojo tournament held 10 February 1935, thus giving Tentoku Kan an unexpectedly easy victory.[35] The promotion ceremony coincided with the opening of Tentoku Kan's new home, which was inside the Murakumo Hall at the Nichiren Buddhist Temple.

Sakata also proved his personal skills as a grappler during a tournament held on 22 September 1935.[36] His specialty was ground wrestling, or *newaza*, something many of the Seattle judoka hadn't practiced much.[37] Said the *Great Northern Daily News* afterward:[38]

> Sakata, who holds a go-dan [fifth black] rank, proved his right to the title by downing ten men in a row in the feature event of the evening. He started out with a win over Frank Takeshita, Kent strongman; and when he had finished, the following had gone down to defeat: Susumu Nitta, Miyake, ni-dans [second black]; George Hiranaka, Takeo Horiuchi, Toregoe, Mas Tominaga, Hiroshi Kato, and younger Nitta sho-dans [first black]; and Ted Takeshita, ikkyu [first brown].

Kuniyuki Kaname, by now ranked 3rd-dan, returned from Japan on 15 December 1935. As Sakata was often out of town on business, Kuniyuki became the usual instructor. One of his first students was fifteen-year-old Katsumi ("Jim") Yoshida. Yoshida did not want to do judo, but his father told him that if he wanted to keep playing football, he would have to learn either judo or kendo. As young Yoshida didn't like the idea of being whacked on the head with a stick, he decided on judo. He chose Tentoku Kan rather than Seattle Dojo because his father was friends with Tad Kuniyuki's father.[40]

There were about two dozen youths training at the Tentoku Kan during the winter of 1935–1936. Classes met Monday, Wednesday, and Friday from 7 p.m. to 9:30 p.m. Training involved learning to kneel Japanese style and throwing and being thrown almost without break. About once a month the Tentoku Kan held an intraclub tournament. These contests were single elimination, with the winners staying up and the losers sitting down. During an internal tournament held in May 1936, Yoshida, who stood about 5'9" and weighed about 170 pounds (approximately six inches taller and forty pounds heavier than his peers), threw seven men in a row, including two black belts. For this feat, he was promoted from white belt to black belt.[41]

After class on Friday nights, if they had money, Yoshida and his friends would go to the Paramount Cafe on Jackson Street, where Pete Fujino's sister worked as a waitress, and eat pie, drink milk, and play the pinball machines with their nickels. If they didn't have money, then they would go to the Nakamura house on Yesler Way, and play penny-ante poker and sing. "We did all the things white kids our age did for fun," Yoshida later told Bill Hosokawa, "but we never forgot we were Japanese-Americans."[42]

Tentoku Kan sponsored its eighth anniversary tournament at the Nippon Kan Theater on 1 March 1936. According to the *Japanese American Courier*, "Three hundred agile athletes, their bulging biceps hidden in the padding of judo jackets, took part."[43] Nitta Masaru, Kato Hiroshi, and Frank Yoshitake won the team title for Tentoku Kan. Kuniyuki Kaname had a disappointing day, however, being thrown by Masato Tamura of Fife during a demonstration match.[44]

Tentoku Kan normally closed during the summer because the young men got jobs in Alaskan fish canneries. Judo men were in demand both as workers (they were usually fitter than other youths were) and as foremen (in these pre-union times, foremen were expected to keep their work gangs in line, physically if necessary). Tentoku Kan men working at the Nakat Packing Corporation cannery in Waterfall, Alaska, in the summer of 1936 included Kuniyuki Kaname, Nitta Susumu, Jim Yoshida, and Koiwai Eichi. "We practiced judo on the wooden floor (no mats) in the warehouse to keep us in top condition," says Koiwai. They also watched movies; played craps; and, on Sundays and Mondays, the Alaskan days of rest, danced with the nisei women employed in the warehouses. "Until we get one choice gal to each man, I know there is no alternative, but to rotate them around," explained George Takigawa in 1940.[46]

Such hijinks only took place when there were no fish, of course. When the boats were in, everyone worked until the fish were processed. Pay was low, overtime was rare, and the food was little but rice and salmon. Still, no one got tired of the diet, in part because only the choicest cuts were eaten. (Indeed, former cannery men still debate which tasted better, the lean cheeks of a sockeye or the fat-laden abdominal steaks of an Alaskan king salmon.) They also supplemented their meager wages of about $75 a month by salting their favorite cuts into wooden boxes, then smuggling their booty home in duffel bags.[47]

Regular training resumed in late August or early September, after the salmon runs ended, and everyone returned to Seattle.[48] By October, everyone was back in shape. In October 1936, twenty three northwest judoka drove to California to participate in a big interstate tournament. In part because they had received their ranks in Japan, Kuniyuki Kaname and Kelly Uno were the northwest team captains. Supervision and planning was provided by Sakata Chuji and Sakano Ichiro of the Tentoku Kan, and Kumagai Yasuyuki and Miyazawa Yasutaro of Seattle Dojo.[49]

As a group, the California judo clubs gave the visitors a cool reception. Said the *Japanese American Courier* upon their return to Seattle: "The traveling team found themselves practically ignored in Los Angeles until Kaz Nishimura, former Seattlite, and Kimon Kudo, Seattle wrestler, came to their rescue."[50] San Francisco judo groups were worse: they ignored the visitors altogether. At an individual level, however, the northwesterners had nothing but praise for the California judoka, and they were especially impressed by the skill of Kano Jigoro, founder of judo, who happened to be in Los Angeles at the time. The actual meet took place in San Pedro on 24–25 October 1936. The match was about even, the California judoka winning Saturday and the northwesterners winning on Sunday. Individual stars included Masato Tamura of Fife and Nitta Susumu of Tentoku Kan. In fact, these two did so well that Professor Kano personally promoted both to 3rd-dan.

"Following the tournament in 1936," says Larry Kobayashi, a longtime student and friend of Kuniyuki Kaname,[51]

> Kuniyuki Sensei was approached by Mr. Jack Wada, an astute businessman on the west side of Los Angeles, to take over the duties of head instructor of Seinan Judo Dojo. Sensei accepted and became the head instructor in 1936. He was also offered the same duties at Uemachi Dojo in the Uptown district. So, Sensei actually taught at the two dojos until the war broke out. At Uemachi, all the students were Japanese-Americans, while at Seinan Dojo the students were mostly Japanese-Americans but occasionally police officers like Jack Sergel (who later acted in a few movies as a Japanese military officer because of his judo background) and other Caucasian students used to come to practice because of our close proximity to the University of Southern California. Because of Sensei's training in Japan, we would have visitors from Japan who worked out at our dojo while in Los Angeles. When Sensei took over Seinan, it was a comparatively weak dojo. Gradually it was transformed into a powerhouse under the teachings of Kuniyuki Sensei.

Above: Tournament at the Nippon Kan Theater on Sunday, 1 February 1934. The lone European American judoka in the back row was probably Stanley MacDonald of the Seattle Dojo. Photo courtesy of Kozu Shinji.

Kobayashi adds: "Kuniyuki Sensei was outstanding in standing wrestling. I've never seen anyone better."[52] This skill was based in part on sweat, and in part on research and study. Says Kobayashi, "He had a lot of books on judo, mostly in Japanese. It was the best collection I've seen."[53]

Meanwhile, back in Seattle, Tentoku Kan hosted a tournament at the Nippon Kan Theater on 13 December 1936. Junior players from Tentoku Kan included Bob and Ben Ikeda, Hayashi Meiji, Higashi Akira, Shibuya Tadao, Tanemura Toshikazu, and Shimada Masayuki. Senior players included Nitta Masaru, Kato Hiroshi, Sumioka Shigeo, Jim Yoshida, Harry Sekiya, Momoda Shigeru, and Mizuki Mitsuo.[54]

Tentoku Kan also gave exhibitions. For example, Shimada Masayuki, Mamiya Sumio, Kato Hiroshi, and Nitta Susuma gave an exhibition to the Veterans of Foreign Wars at the Green Lake Fieldhouse on Wednesday, 31 January 1937. The club even took its entire cast of black belts to the Seattle YMCA on Sunday, 17 January 1938. There members gave demonstrations and explained that judo prepared one not just for self-defense but for life as well. And on Friday, 21 May 1938, Tentoku Kan supported a judo and kendo exhibition at the American Legion Hall. Judoka taking part in this show included Sakata Chuji, T. Bun, Mamiya Satoru, and Tsuchikawa Kiyoshi.[55] As the American Legion was usually very anti-Japanese, the show was undoubtedly meant to ease tensions between the Legion and Japanese-Americans.

Tentoku Kan held its ninth anniversary tournament at the Nippon Kan Theater on Sunday, 14 February 1937. The Japanese consul and the president of the Japanese Association spoke on behalf of the community, while Sakata Chuji and K. Yoshitake spoke on behalf of the judo club. Joe Nakatsu, of Tentoku Kan's Sunnydale branch, was also honored as the first Japanese-American to earn a varsity letter at Highline High School in Des Moines, Washington (large for a nisei, he played halfback.)[56]

"Joe was about as big as Pete [Fujino], and we met through judo," Jim Yoshida recalled.[57]

> Joe didn't say much, but we got along famously. He and I were usually the top boys in judo tournaments, which meant that often we faced each other. In one match we were fooling around, each not wanting to throw the other, and the referee was about to call it a draw when Joe's dad jumped up and shouted: "Yoshida, if you're good enough to throw my son, I want you to throw him and win." Well, we both went at it, and I threw Joe. As soon as he hit the mat Joe jumped up and embraced me, and I cried because I had defeated my friend. We were that kind of buddies.

Of course, such parental behavior sometimes embarrassed the young men to whom it was directed. One Tentoku Kan father was notorious for yelling at Seattle Dojo officials during tournaments. A Seattle Dojo judoka asked the man's son if this behavior didn't bother him. The son replied that it embarrassed him tremendously, but that there was nothing he could do to stop his father from yelling that wouldn't hurt the man's feelings. And, as there weren't many places that this hard-working farmer could vent his frustrations, his son didn't feel right telling him to restrain himself at tournament.[58] To minimize such unseemly behavior, both Mr. Kumagai and Mr. I Sakata worked hard at judging matches so fairly that there would be no reason for anyone to complain. This explains much of their popularity with the parents and players of both Tentoku Kan and Seattle Dojo.

A California judo team visited Seattle in April 1937. The meet was held at the Seattle Chamber of Commerce hall on 3–4 April 1937. The northwest judoka won 7–6 in team competition, but lost 11–9 in individual competition. Tentoku Kan judoka who won their individual matches in this tournament included Torigoye Kanezo and Nitta Masaru.[59]

On Sunday, 12 December 1937, White River Dojo held its tenth anniversary tournament at the White River Buddhist Temple in Auburn. Higashi of Tentoku Kan won first place in the senior division while Kitajima of Green Lake took first in the junior.[60]

With such a record, Tentoku Kan went to the Nippon Kan Theater on 24 January 1938 intending to keep the team pennant it had won the year before. However, its members went home disappointed. While Jim Yoshida made it to the semi-finals, no Tentoku Kan player made it any further. Meanwhile, Bainbridge Island took first in senior team competition while Green Lake took first in junior.[61]

The Tentoku Kan hosted its tenth anniversary tournament at the Nippon Kan Theater on 27 February 1938. Having started with just twenty players in

1928, ten years later, counting its affiliates in Bellevue, Kent, and Sunnydale, it now boasted more than one hundred players.[62] Although they had not done well during the Seattle Dojo's thirty-first anniversary tournament two weeks before, Tentoku Kan players outdid themselves in this tournament, winning three of the top five spots in the senior competition.

Bellevue players dominated the junior division. Tom Okazaki, 2nd dan, especially distinguished himself during the team competition by throwing two men and drawing with a third.[63]

The *Seattle Post-Intelligencer* sent a reporter to this tournament. Afterward, the reporter wrote, "Judo's purposes as explained by Coach Sakata of Seattle, is manifold: to develop the body, to develop character, and to protect oneself."[64] Photographs showing Koiwai Eichi of Tentoku Kan throwing Ted Hachiya of Portland accompanied the article.[65]

Kano Jigoro flew into Seattle on Tuesday, 19 April 1938. He was on his way back to Japan from International Olympic Committee meetings that had been held in Greece and Egypt. Meeting him at Boeing Field were Kumagai Yasuyuki of Seattle Dojo and Sakata Chuji of Tentoku Kan. The next day, Kano ate dinner at the Gyokko Ken as the guest of the Seattle Yudanshakai (Black Belt Association). Afterward, Kano watched a judo exhibition at Washington Hall, and awarded various promotions, including a 2nd-dan ranking for Koiwai Eichi. Kano died on 4 May 1938, and Sakata Chuji sent the Seattle judokas' condolences to Kano's family in Tokyo.[66]

In November 1938, Sakata Chuji left Seattle. His employer may have transferred him to Los Angeles. This left Hama Hideo (3rd-dan) as chief instructor at Tentoku Kan. Hama's assistants included Torigoe Kanezo, Kato Hiroshi, Tom Okazaki, Sumioka Shigeo, and Elmer Tazumaa[67] Despite Sakata absence, Tentoku Kan went to the third annual Yudanshakai tournament two weeks later in Seattle and took second overall. Jim Yoshida was the individual Tentoku Kan star of this tournament, making it to the quarterfinals before losing to Masato Tamura of Eatonville.[68]

Sakata was in Los Angeles for the February 1939 all-star tournament. Tentoku Kan leaders accompanying the team included Hama Hideo (3rd-dan). Leading Tentoku Kan players on the all-star squad included Kato Hiroshi (3rd dan), Jim Yoshida (2nd-dan), and Joe Nakatsu (2nd-dan). The Tentoku Kan players did not enjoy any individual success in California: Joe Nakatsu got a draw, and Jim Yoshida and Kato Hiroshi lost to the Californians on Saturday, 4 March 1939. However, they were part of the team victory the following day, and so got to fondle the 36" high trophy that commemorated the win. On the way back, they also made a side trip to visit the World's Fair in San Francisco.[69]

Tentoku Kan hosted its eleventh anniversary tournament at the Nippon Kan Theater on Sunday, 19 February 1939. This was the first tournament attended by Tentoku Kan's Spokane affiliate. And a good thing, too, as otherwise Tentoku Kan would have lost almost all their trophies to Seattle Dojo affiliates.[70]

Nitta Susumu, who had gone to Japan in 1937, returned home ranked 4th-dan in September 1939, making him Tentoku Kan's highest-ranking nisei judoka (while Hama Hideo was 3rd-dan, he was also issei, which gave him cultural seniority). Nitta's welcome home banquet was held at Seattle's Nikko Low restaurant on Sunday, 24 September 1939.[71] Nitta, who was known to his friends as "Baby Beef" (his even brawnier older brother Masaru was "Beefo"), remained active in northwest judo following his return, and soon became supervisor at Tentoku Kan's Bellevue, Sunnydale, and Kent affiliate.[72]

Below: The Northwest Judo All Star Team in Los Angeles, 1939.
Photo courtesy of Masato Tamura Collection.

On 15 December 1939, Yorita Tatsuo, another Tentoku Kan 4th-dan, also returned to Seattle from Japan.[73] Like Nitta, Yorita was initially active in dojo activities, but unlike Nitta, his involvement didn't last long, as he found himself engaged to Yonemura Yoshiko of Wapato in October 1940, and married soon after.[74] Tentoku Kan's twelfth anniversary tournament was held in Seattle on Sunday, 4 February 1940.[75] The results were not listed in the Seattle newspapers. About the same time, the Nichiren Temple moved, and the club moved with it.

The Seattle Dojo's thirty-third anniversary tournament took place three weeks later. The champion in the 2nd-dan competition was Jim Yoshida, whom the *North American Times* described as "another who relied principally on his physical prowess."[76] Hank Ogawa of Bainbridge Island, who was Yoshida's friendly opponent during those days, adds, "You didn't try to sweep him. He was too big. His legs were like tree trunks."[77]

During Seattle's fifth annual yudanshakai tournament on Sunday, 10 November 1940, Jim Yoshida won another individual championship and the Consul's Cup. In junior competition, Ikeda (its unclear whether it was Bob or Ben), Komorita Shozo, Nitta Masaru, and Shibuya Tadao also placed first or second in their divisions.[78]

Tentoku Kan's thirteenth anniversary tournament was held in Seattle on 23 February 1941.[79] Soon after, Jim Yoshida accompanied his mother on a trip to Japan, where she was taking his father's ashes for burial. While there, Yoshida studied judo at the Kodokan. There was no horseplay at the Kodokan in 1941, Yoshida said, "only intense, dedicated concentration on judo."[80] Training lasted eight hours a day, six and a half days a week, with fifteen-minute breaks for lunch. On the mat:[81]

> Anyone could come up to you and request a practice bout. . . [and] the rule was that you couldn't refuse. . . Eventually, as I worked out day after day, the truth of what Kenny Kuniyuki had tried to teach dawned on me: Judo is not a test of strength alone; judo is a sport of skill and its essence is timing.

Of course, all was not hardship. Otherwise no one would have done it. Instead, said the English judoka Trevor Leggett, who left the Kodokan in 1940, when the teacher was in the room, then the formality and solemnity were palpable, and hardly a word was exchanged anywhere. But once the teacher left the room for his bath:[82]

> Immediately everyone relaxes, and their natural Japanese cheerfulness comes out. The practice is over, and you can smoke and talk freely, and joke as much as you like. In the next room is a huge bath of steaming hot water where one can soak, and afterwards return to cool off clad in nothing but a towel. Some tea and cakes are brought in, and you spend a pleasant half hour with some of the jolliest, kindest, and most unaffected friends you could meet anywhere in the world.

Shortly before he was scheduled to return to the United States in August 1941, Yoshida threw a line of Japanese Navy 3rd-dans who had come to the Kodokan seeking promotion. As a result, Yoshida was rewarded with promotion to 4th-dan. Unfortunately, the Japanese preparations for the attack on Pearl Harbor interfered with Yoshida's plans for returning to the United States, and after a year teaching judo in a Japanese high school, he found himself serving in a Japanese artillery unit in China. As a result, Yoshida did not get his American citizenship back until 1953.

Tentoku Kan's final tournament appearance took place in Seattle on Sunday, 16 November 1941. The occasion was the third annual Kumagai Cup competition, which honored the memory of Seattle Dojo's Kumagai Yasuyuki, who had returned to Japan in 1940. While Dick Yamasaki of Seattle Dojo won the cup, Tentoku Kan tied with Bainbridge Island for second place in the junior team competition. Fourteen-year old Komorita Shozo was Tentoku Kan's star player of the day.[83]

Like most Japanese-American athletic organizations, Tentoku Kan closed following Pearl Harbor. Starting in May 1942, Seattle's Japanese-Americans began to be sent to a temporary assembly center located at the Puyallup Fairgrounds.

In August 1942, the internees started relocating from Puyallup to Hunt, Idaho. As Minidoka Camp was still under construction and mates were not available, formal judo classes did not resume until 14 February, 1943. Tentoku Kan judoka, including Nitta Masaru, Nitta Susuma, and Sakano Ichiro, were at the forefront of the plan to turn Recreation Halls 5, 17, and 39 into dojos.[84] Jackets were always something of a problem, however, as the younger players outgrew their old jackets while in camp, and new jackets were not commercially available. And while new jackets could be sewn using white canvas duck, such jackets were rarely as strong as prewar commercial uniforms.[85]

Wartime judo training at Minidoka was geared mostly for building character in school-aged boys, as after mid-1943, most older judoka went into military service or found agricultural work outside the camps. The agricultural work was physically demanding and paid terribly (depending on one's skills, wages averaged $12–$14 a month), but it beat sitting inside a prison camp with nothing to do. Meanwhile, military service attracted eight hundred Minidoka nisei, which was more than any other relocation center. Tentoku Kan judoka were especially well-represented among both the volunteers and the casualties.[86]

Above: Interior of the Kodokan 1935. There were no classes at the Kodokan in 1935. Instead, you walked up to anyone you wanted (or dared) and asked him to show you a technique or to grapple. Photo courtesy of Kosu Shinji.

Although Tentoku Kan did not reopen in Seattle following the war, afterwards, its members helped spread judo throughout the United States. For example, Jim Yoshida helped introduce judo into Honolulu high schools. Ken Kuniyuki became a leader in the Nanka Kodokan Judo Yudanshakai in southern California. Koiwai Eichi was active in establishing judo in Philadelphia, and later became a leader in Shufu Yudanshakai and US Judo Inc. Locally, Nitta Susumu also played a key role in the reestablishment of the Seattle Dojo.

Notes on Reference

Research was supported by the King County Landmarks and Heritage Commission and Hotel/Motel Tax Revenues. Research was conducted at the National Archives and Record Administration in Seattle, the Sno-Isle Public Libraries, and the Suzzallo-Allen Libraries at the University of Washington. The assistance of the following individuals is gratefully acknowledged: Fujiko Tamura Gardner, Al C. Holtmann, William K. Hosokawa, S. Chris Kato, Larry Kobayashi, Koiwai Eichi, Kojima Tats, Art Koura, Kozu Shinji, Tad Kuniyuki, Patrick Lineberger, Tom T. Matsuoka, Hank Ogawa, Robert W. Smith, Suzuki Yanagimachi Nobu, Elmer S. Tazuma, D.B. Waterhouse, Yaguchi Kenji, Yamanaka Toshio, and Richard I. Yamasaki.

Endnotes

1. The Zaidan Honin Dai Nippon Butokukai ("Federation of Greater Japan Martial Virtue Society") was established in Kyoto in 1895. Its leaders were as a group more nationalistic and militaristic than the leaders of the Kodokan, and as a result, the Butokukai was closed following the war. The organization encouraged Japanese youth to practice all martial arts, not just judo, and as a stylistic rule, Butokukai judoka emphasized ground grappling (*newma*) while Kodokan judoka emphasized standing grappling (*tachiwaza*). For additional details, see Jeffrey L. Dann, "Kendo in Japanese Martial Culture: Swordsmanship as Self-Cultivation," Ph.D dissertation, University of Washington, 1978, 62–63, fn. 61, 119.
2. *Japanese American Courier*, 29 Sep 1928, 2; *Japanese American Courier*, 13 Oct 1928, 2; *Japanese American Courier*, 26 Feb 1938–4.
3. *Japanese American Courier*, 7 Jan 1928, 2; *Japanese American Courier*, 21 Jan 1928, 2; *Japanese American Courier*, 16 Jun 1928, 2; Letter from Tom T. Matsuoka, 9 Jul 1997.
4. Politics: Interview with S. Chris Kato, 28 Mar 1997; Matsuoka letter, 9 Jul 1997; Name-calling: Interview with Art Koura, 3 May 1997.
5. *North American Times*, 28 Jun 1938, 1.
6. *Japanese American Courier*, 7 Jan 1928, 2.
7. Letter from Tad Kuniyuki, 16 Jun 1997.
8. *Japanese American Courier*, 29 Mar 1930, 2; *Japanese American Courier*, 26 Feb 1938, 4.
9. *Japanese American Courier*, 24 Jan 1931, 2.
10. *Japanese American Courier*, 2 May 1931, 2.
11. Letter from Koiwai Eichi, 12 Jul 1997.
12. *Japanese American Courier*, 21 Feb 1931, 2. While the *Courier* usually called the club "Tentokwan," and the *Great Northern Daily News* called it "Tentokukwan," Polk's City Directory for 1940 shows the club's name as "Tentoku Kan." For consistency, I have used the latter transliteration. Canadian scholar D.B. Waterhouse, of the University of Toronto's East Asian Studies Department, says *kwan* "is an old-fashioned romanisation of Japanese, reflecting the

old-fashioned pronunciation of that syllable." Letter from D.B. Waterhouse, 23 Jul 1997.
13. Waterhouse letter, 23 Jul 1997.
14. While the establishment of the Seattle Dojo is traditionally dated 1907, there were qualified jujutsu instructors living in Seattle at least a decade earlier. Sakamoto Osamu, father of newspaper editor James Y. Sakamoto, is Seattle's first qualified jujutsu instructor of whom I am aware.
15. E.J. Harrison, *The Fighting Spirit of Japan* (New York: Overlook Press, 1982), 51.
16. *Japanese American Courier*, 5 Mar 1932, 2.
17. *Japanese American Courier*, 15 Oct 1932, 2.
18. Harrison, 1982, 47.
19. *Japanese American Courier*, 15 Jul 1933, 2.
20. *Great Northern Daily News*, 17 Oct 1934, 8.
21. *Japanese American Courier*, 14 Jan 1933, 2.
22. *Geat Northern Daily News*, 11 Feb 1935, 8; *North American Times*, 21 Feb 1935, 1.
23. *Japanese American Courier*, 30 Jun 1934, 4; *Japanese American Courier*, 15 Dec 1934, 3.
24. Letter from Kozu Shinji, 22 May 1997.
25. Letter from Kozu Shinji, 31 May 1997.
26. Ibid. Hank Ogawa (31 May 1997 interview) and Yaguchi Kenji (22 Jun 1997 interview) concur with this observation.
27. Letter from Elmer S. Tazuma, 21 May 1997.
28. Interview with Suzuki Yanagimachi Nobu, 31 May 1997.
29. *University of Washington Daily*, 21 Oct 1937, 4. The public baths, or *firoya*, in the basement of the NP Hotel in Seattle had male attendants in the male sections.
30. *Great Northern Daily News*, 20 Feb 1935, 8; *Great Northern Daily News*, 4 Mar 1935, 8.
31. *Great Northern Daily News*, 11 Mar 1935, 8.
32. *Great Northern Daily News*, 14 Mar 1935, 8; *Great Northern Daily News*, 15 Mar 1935, 8.
33. "List or Manifest of Alien Passengers for the U.S. Immigration Officer at Port of Arrival," Heian Maru, 14 May 1935, M1383; "Passenger and Crew Lists of Vessels Arriving at Seattle, Washington, 1891–1957," Roll 204, Apr 22, 1935, Screw Beatrice – June 1, 1935, SS Tantalus.
34. *Great Northern Daily News*, 15 May 1935, 8; *Great Northern Daily News*, 24 May 1935, 8.

Many years later, Sakata told Kazuo Ito: "I graduated from Tokyo Fisheries Institute. I gave judo lessons to nisei and sansei youths at Seattle. . . . At that time Japanese were living shrunken lives under the storm of anti-Japanese feeling. The tall white men frequently insulted the Japanese with their small body and mind by saying, 'Harro Chary!' and roughing up our hair. . . [But I] am 5'5" tall, and I was never insulted or excluded. My ears were cauliflowered due to hard training. Noticing them, whites always said: 'Are you a wrestler?' 'No, I'm a professor of judo.' 'You strong man! Shake hands!' In Kazuo Ito, *Issei: A History of Japanese Immigrants in North America*, translated by Shinichiro Nakamura and Jean S. Gerard (Seattle: Japanese Community Service, 1973), 133.

35 *Great Northern Daily News*, 11 Feb 1935, 2.
36 *Great Northern Daily News*, 21 Sep 1935, 8.
37 Koiwai letter, 12 Jul 1997.
38 *Great Northern Daily News*, 23 Sep 1935, 8.
39 *Japanese American Courier*, 21 Dec 1935, 3.
40 Jim Yoshida with Bill Hosokawa, *The Two Worlds of Jim Yoshida* (New York: William Morrow, 1972), 24–25.
41 Ibid., 26–27.
42 Ibid., 18–20.
43 *Japanese American Courier*, 7 Mar 1936, 3; *Japanese American Courier*, 9 Mar 1935, 3; *Japanese American Courier*, 16 Mar 1935, 3.
44 Masato Tamura collection.
45 Koiwai letter, 12 Jul 1997.
46 *Great Northern Daily News*, 14 Aug 1940's. See also *Great Northern Daily News*, 13 Aug 1940, 8.
47 During the 1930s, about seven hundred Seattle nisei spent their summers working in Alaskan or Aleutian canneries. Base pay was about $90–$100 a month, from which living expenses were deducted. In 1940, overtime (at $.90 an hour) was paid employees who worked eight hours on Sunday, or more than sixteen consecutive hours a day; Interview with Hank Ogawa, 31 May 1997; *North American Times*, 25 May 1940, 1; Paul Yee, *Saltwater City: An Illustrated History of the Chinese in Vancouver* (Seattle: University of Washington, 1988), 59, 62–63; Yoshida, 1972, 28.
48 *Great Northern Daily News*, 6 Sep 1941, 8.
49 *Japanese American Courier*, 24 Oct 1936, 3.
50 *Japanese American Courier*, 7 Nov 1936, 3.
51 Letter from Larry Kobayashi, 19 Aug 1997.
52 Interview with Larry Kobayashi, 8 Aug 1997.
53 Ibid.
54 *Japanese American Courier*, 12 Dec 1936, 3.
55 Tsuchikawa's younger brother "Mud" (Masakatsu) was Jim Yoshida's friend, and another Tentoku Kan junior player.
56 *Japanese American Courier*, 13 Feb 1937, 3. A photograph of Nakatsu Jintaro's family, in which Joe Nakatsu appears fifth from the right, appears in the book, *Hokubei Nenkan*, lower plate [32], which is located in the University of Washington's East Asia Library. The call number is N979.5N79y.
57 Yoshida, 1972, 18–19.
58 For obvious reasons, the individual who told me this story requested anonymity

for all concerned. The interview was conducted 27 Jul 1997.
59 *Japanese American Courier*, 3 Apr 1937, 3; *Japanese American Courier*, 10 Apr 1937, 3.
60 *Great Northern Daily News*, 13 Dec 1937, 8; *North American Times*, 8 Dec 1937, 1.
61 *Great Northern Daily News*, 24 Jan 1938, 8.
62 *Japanese American Courier*, 26 Feb 1938, 4; *North American Times*, 26 Feb 1938, 1.
63 *Great Northern Daily News*, 7 Feb 1938, 8; *Great Northern Daily News*, 22 Feb 1938, 8; *North American Times*, 7 Feb 1938, 1; *North American Times*, 28 Feb 1938, 1. Okazaki died in France during World War II.
64 *Seattle Post-Intelligencer*, 20 Mar 1938, 5.
65 Koiwai letter, 12 Jul 1997.
66 *Japanese American Courier*, 23 Apr 1938, 4; *Japanese American Courier*, 7 May 1938, 3; *Japanese American Courier*, 14 Sep 1940, 4; Koiwai letter, 12 Jul 1997.
67 *Great Northern Daily News*, 7 Nov 1938, 8.
68 *Great Northern Daily News*, 21 Nov 1938, 8.
69 *North American Times*, 6 Mar 1939, 1; *North American Times*, 11 Mar 1939, 1; *North American Times*, 13 Mar 1939, 1.
70 *North American Times*, 16 Feb 1939, 1; *North American Times*, 18 Feb 1939, 1.
71 This was a Chinese restaurant rather than a Japanese restaurant. Letter from William K. Hosokawa, 4 Sep 1997.
72 *Japanese American Courier*, 23 Sep 1939, 3; *North American Times*, 22 Sep 1939, 1 ; *North American Times*, 23 Jan 1939, 1; *North American Times*, 10 Jan 1940, 1.
73 *North American Times*, 14 Dec 1939, 1.
74 *Great Northern Daily News*, 19 Oct 1940, 8.
75 *North American Times*, 31 Jan 1940, 1.
76 *North American Times*, 26 Feb 1940, 1.
77 Ogawa interview, 31 May 1997; Letter from Toshio Yamanaka, 17 Sep 1997.
78 *North American Times*, 11 Nov 1940, 1.
79 *Great Northern Daily News*, 20 Feb 1941, 8.
80 Yoshida, 1972, 41.
81 Ibid., 42.
82 *Japanese American Courier*, 28 Sep 1940, 3.
83 *Great Northern Daily News*, 17 Nov 1941, 8.
84 *Minidoka Irrigator*, 27 Feb 1943, 7. "Many of the builders," says historian Leonard Arrington, "coming from farms rather than cities, lived in houses and shacks without running water, and they used outhouses. As they constructed the camp's communal kitchens, laundries, and bathhouses they were envious: the incoming 'Japs' were being given such 'luxuries' as public toilets at public expense. It would never have occurred to the workers what a God-forsaken place this would seem to people from Portland and Seattle forcibly exiled into the Idaho desert." Leonard J. Arrington, *History of Idaho*, vol. 11 (Moscow, ID:

University of Idaho Press, 1994), 88.

[85] Conversation with Fujiko Gardner, 7 Jun 1997; interview with S. Chris Kato, 28 Mar 1997; Koiwai letter, 12 Jul 1997; Ogawa interview, 31 May 1997; "Jiu-Jitsu Institute," two letters in "Henry H. Okuda," Accession Number 2345, Box 1, University of Washington Manuscripts and University Archives Division, University of Washington, Seattle, WA.

[86] Ibid.; Arrington, 1994, 88–92.

American Judo Pioneer Vince Tamura & Heike-ryu Jujutsu

James Webb, M.A.

All photos courtesy of Vince Tamura, except where noted.

Introduction

The name Vince Tamura is synonymous with the growth and establishment of judo in America. Among his firsts were his being chosen as the "A" player (a top player in the country) to represent the United States at the First World Championship of Judo (Tokyo, 1956) and his further being chosen to be a referee at the introduction of judo to the Olympic Games (Tokyo, 1964). The U.S. team was made up of Paul Maruyama, Jim Bregman (who took bronze), George Harris, and Ben Campbell.

Vince Tamura's legacy can be readily seen today through the many champions he has produced, a tournament that still draws the some of the toughest players in the world, and a revitalized jujutsu (sometimes written as "jiujitsu") system. His family story, going back hundreds of years, shows a strong lineage of people making an impact on history.

History of the Taira Clan

The roots of the Tamura family can be found in ancient Japan. The two most influential clans vying for control of Japan during the end of the Heian period (784–1184) were the Taira and Minamoto. Vince Tamura is a descendent of the Taira clan. Takami, the grandson of the Emperor Kammu, first adopted the name Taira. Emperor Kammu (r. 781–806) founded Kyoto.

"Genji" is the Sino-Japanese pronunciation of the written character that the Japanese read as "Minamoto." In the same way, the Taira are often referred to as the Heike. This has always resulted in some confusion to idle observers of Japanese history. For while the Taira went on to control Japan, the novel written by the famous author Eiji Yoshikawa describing the clans story was called *The Tale of the Heike*.

As the two clans rose in military strength and political influence, it became inevitable that they would clash. Unfortunately, throughout the Gempei War (1180–1185), the situation of the Taira clan grew progressively worse until the final battle of Dannoura, which marked the utter destruction of the Taira as they were driven into the sea. The most tragic event was enacted by Nii-no-Ama, the grandmother of the infant Emperor Antoku who, when confronted with the alternative of surrendering to the warriors of the Minamoto clan, clasped the child tightly in her arms and plunged into waves of the straits, followed by the other court ladies. So complete was the defeat that the name Taira temporarily disappeared from Japanese history, leaving the site to be more renown for ghost stories of fallen samurai bent on revenge.

The best known legend from the battle concerns the Heike crabs, which are said to contain within their shells the spirits of the dead samurai. Their shells do indeed bear the shape of a human face, when viewed with an active imagination.

Heike-ryu Jujutsu

Not all of the members of the Taira clan perished in the final series of battles. Those descendants of Taira Kiyomori that managed to survive the final wrath of the Minamoto fled to the hills. They would remain there perfecting their samurai skills for a day of revenge that would never surface. Vince's mother, a direct descendent of Taira Kiyomori, remained in Japan until her death in Yamaguchi-ken, Honshu Prefecture.

One of the skills that had been handed down through the family for generations was the Tamura family jujutsu style: Heike-ryu.

The symbol of Heike-ryu Jujutsu shows the Heike crab returning from the sea. Two American brothers, well-known in both judo and jujutsu circles, have surfaced from this tradition: Mas and Vince Tamura. While many modern coaches have abandoned the original roots of judo in pursuit of mastering the Olympic sport, the Tamura family has continually encouraged students to study jujutsu to master not only the self-defense aspects but also the roots of the martial art and the warrior spirit (*bushido*). It is important to note that the ancient style of Heike-ryu jujutsu had been dormant for many years until the brothers revitalized the art with modern techniques.

The style is called Heike-ryu Jujutsu mostly out of respect for the family history as it bears little resemblance to the jujutsu style of ancient Japan. The old Heike-ryu techniques were developed for the samurai to be used while in armor and on the field of battle. Modern techniques have been adapted from these roots to be practical in a more modern environment with street clothes.

While many of the throws and grappling techniques resemble those of Kodokan judo, an equally large number of techniques come from the more traditional jujutsu lineage—those techniques such as wrist locks and striking techniques that are illegal in judo competition but have been found to be effective in a modern hostile environment.

Vince Tamura throwing brother Mas
with "floating throw" (*uki otoshi*) (1957).

Vince Tamura's Role in the Growth of American Judo

Vince's older brother, Mas Tamura, grew into a formidable judo competitor in his hometown of Fife, Washington, under the direction of Iwakiri Ryochi. Iwakiri had a produce business but had learned judo in Japan and had volunteered this skill to the community. Kumagai Yasuyuki was also instrumental in molding this program as he was an instructor sent by the Kodokan.

In 1936, Professor Kano Jigoro (the founder of Kodokan Judo) saw Mas win the individual competition of a large tournament held in Seattle, Washington. Kano was so impressed with the abilities of the competitor that he personally promoted Mas Tamura to 3rd-degree black belt. Mas' success in judo had a profound effect upon his younger brother. To this day, Vince still greatly admires Mas.

The Fife Dojo was the result of the Japanese community building a school to ensure that their children captured their Japanese roots. At the far end of the school, a dojo was built, separated from the remainder of the school by a sliding door, and boasting the traditional mat fashioned from woven rice straw (*tatami*).

The youngest and seventh son, Vince remembers his early tournaments as his being "first up, first down." He started judo at a very young age, and, being the smallest, he started at the beginning of the traditional line-up tournaments (where competitors lined up along the side of the mat by size and skill and fought until they lost). Vince usually lost his first match to older and stronger competitors. His first judo match was in 1933 at the age of four.

Vince Tamura wins the 1957 Midwestern Championships in Detroit, Michigan. The win was memorable for Vince as he defeated the very tough and established John Osako in the final.

With the outbreak of World War II, the Tamura family was relocated to the assembly center at Camp Harmony in Puyallup, Washington. Not all of the memories here were bitter; however, as many days spent practicing judo and sumo finally paid off for Vince as he won his first tournament—the award being a coveted pocketknife.

In 1941, Mas moved to Illinois to take over the reins of Chicago's Jiujitsu Institute. There he found a serious test in 1943 when the *Chicago Times* encouraged a match between the 216-pound international wrestler Karl Pojello and the 143-pound Tamura. The audience was primarily made up of the top athletic officers of the Armed Forces and notables such as Avery Bundage, the head of the Olympic Committee. Mas won the match in one minute twenty seconds by rendering Pojello unconscious. Mas taught in Chicago for thirty-one years and died in 1982.

Above: Vince Tamura "attacking the inside of the thigh" (*uchi-mata*) at the 1958 Nationals in Chicago.

Vince joined Mas in Chicago at the Jiujitsu Institute at the age of fourteen. Chicago area judo quickly grew as other instructors left the relocation camps for Chicago: John Osako (Chicago Judo Club), Henry Okamura (Lawson YMCA—usually where the competitions were held), and Hic Nagao (University of Chicago). Bill Kaufman migrated from the Jiujitsu Institute to start a club at the Evanston YMCA.

Below: Vince Tamura squares off against Ken Hatae in the finals of the 1959 US National Championships in San Jose, California. Ken Hatae was a recent arrival from Japan, where he was the captain of his university judo team, and was training in San Jose. Vince won the match and the National Championship.

No longer "first up, first down," Vince entered one tournament in which eight black belts formed the black belt division (this was an unusually large number of black belts at the time) and Vince defeated them all to earn his 3rd-degree black belt.

The second US National Championships was held in San Francisco in 1954. Vince Tamura won the tournament. He went on to win the US Nationals three times. In the seven years of his active competition, he never failed to place in the top three.

It was little wonder that Vince Tamura was chosen to represent the United States at the First World Judo Championship in 1956. He made it to the semi-final, losing a close match to Anton Geesink, the future world champion from The Netherlands. The honor was noteworthy as there was only one division contested during that time. The "B" player from the United States, the more established Mitsuo Kimura, drew a tough Frenchman by the name of Cortine and went out in the first round.

The World Championships was Vince's second visit to Japan. On his first visit, he was returning from serving in the Korean war (where he received a Bronze Star for bravery in action) and stopped in Japan to visit his relatives in Honshu. He stopped by the Kodokan to work out and met Donn Draeger (whom he had known in Chicago) and one of his brother's friends, Tomonari. Through Tomonari, Mifune Kyuzo (1883–1965, one of the famous Kodokan 10th-degree black belts) had given Vince a judo uniform to take back to Mas as a gift. Mas was the president of the Chicago Yudanshakai (black belt association) at that time. At the end of a long, hard workout, Vince remembers that he could not walk up the few steps to his hotel room and had to crawl on his hands and knees.

Vince returned to Chicago to live in an apartment complex and found Ms. Shiratori Yuri living in the same complex. Jim Colgan (now an 8th-degree black belt still living in Chicago) claims that Yuri was one of the most beautiful girls he had ever seen. Vince soon married her.

Vince's second visit to Japan, and the World Championship, found his introduction to Ms. Fukuda Keiko, who was contemplating a move to the United States at the time. She moved to California shortly thereafter and began to teach excellence in kata. Fukida is the granddaughter of Fukuda Hachinosuke. Kano Jigoro studied Tenshin Shinyo-ryu jujutsu under Hachinosuke before founding the Kodokan.

Left: Action in Chicago in 1960. The competitor on the left is Vince Tamura. The referee is John Osako.

The Chicago Team attends the 1960 Nationals — Front row (left to right): Vince Tamura, George Colgan, Curtis Belmont, Jim Colgan. Second row: Fred Jorgensen, Bill Kaufman, Ed Ernst, Rhett Summerville. Back row: Henry Okamura, Hik Nagao, Masato Tamura, and John Osako.

With the start of a family, Vince found that his two young boys (David and Bob) had trouble coping with the harsh Chicago winters and sought warmer climates. Finding themselves in Florida for the US National Championships, Vince and Yuri thought that would be great place to live—until a hurricane hit. They then headed west, enjoying the hospitality of Jaques LeGrand (a Frenchman who had fought Vince in several national championships) in New Orleans along the way. Eventually, they made it to Dallas, Texas, where one of the buildings downtown reminded Vince of Chicago. This became their new home, and Vince quickly opened a judo school.

His first school was located next to a bar called The Doll House. The bar owner learned to both love and hate having the judo school next door. On the one hand, some of his best customers were judo students. On the other hand, very often a student would be thrown into the common wall and glasses would be knocked over.

In the Texas Yudanshakai, Vince found some great company: Bill Nagase and Sam Numajiri were in Fort Worth, Fred Usui had come from Hawaii to open a club in the Dallas Downtown YMCA, Gail Stolzenburg was in Austin with Pop Moore, Karl Geis was in Houston, Eddie Elizalde was in San Antonio with Herb Bellamy, and Tim Joe was in Amarillo. Typically shunning political positions, Vince eventually agreed to become the chairman of the Texas Yudanshakai Board of Examiners—a position now held by Vince's longtime student, Jim Webb.

With 1964 came the Olympic Games in Tokyo and Vince's return to Japan to be a referee in the judo competition. While there, Olympic team members Jim Bregman and George Harris remarked on what a great help Vince was in helping them prepare for the Games. Jim Bregman captured the bronze medal.

TECHNICAL SECTION

Defense Against a Knife

The defender moves away from the direction of the knife lunge, while bringing his hands up to grab the attacker's right wrist. He then pushes the attacker's fingers back toward his elbow, forcing the attacker's hand to loosen its grip on the knife. Stepping back with the left foot, the defender twists the attacker's bent wrist to the outside to throw the attacker.

Note the focus remains on controlling the knife throughout the technique until the weapon is taken from the attacker or used to injure the attacker. James Webb acts as the attacker in this technical section, with Vince Tamura showing the defense techniques. *Photography in this section courtesy of P. Robbins.*

Defense Against a Gun from the Rear

Turn the body out of the line of fire while bringing up the arm up to lock the attacker's elbow. Apply pressure to the attacker's elbow and drive him to the ground while maintaining control of the weapon at all times.

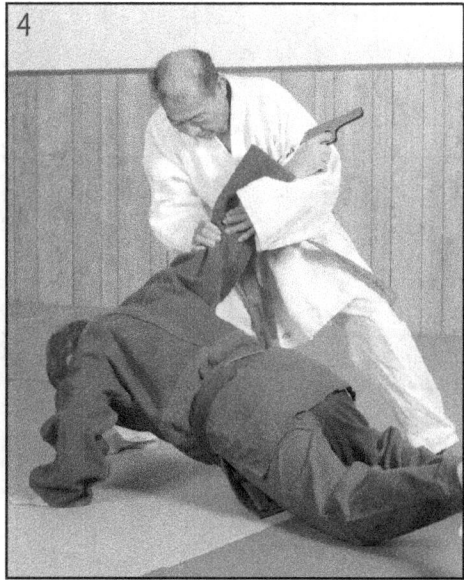

Defense Against an Overhand Knife Strike

The defender blocks with the left hand while bringing his right hand up behind the attacker's arm and around to the attacker's wrist. With the attacker's arm bent, the defender leverages the forearm to throw the attacker to the ground. The defender continues to apply pressure to the arm until the attacker releases the weapon.

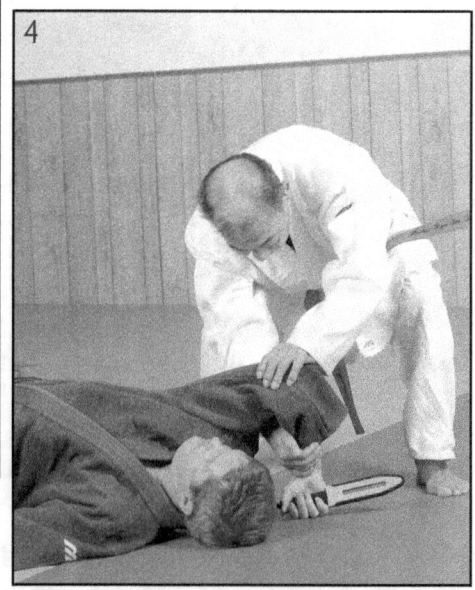

Defense Against an Overhead Club Strike

The defender steps forward with the left foot while simultaneously blocking with his left hand. The right hand pushes the attacker's shoulder back and down while the right leg sweeps the attacker's leg, throwing him to the ground. The defender locks the attacking arm with a figure four arm bar until the attacker releases the weapon.

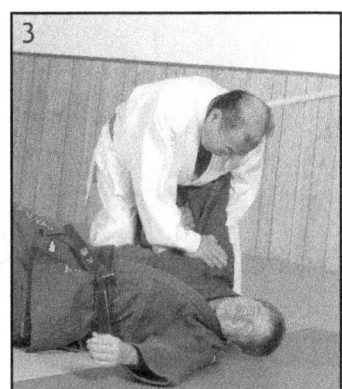

Conclusion

Since opening the dojo in Dallas, Vince won the National Masters Championship for fourteen consecutive years before retiring from competition. He also founded and oversaw the Dallas Invitational Judo Championship that just held its 37th annual event and has risen to become one of the toughest elite athlete competitions in the country. He has also produced many national and international champions. Most recently, longtime students Ryan and Reno Reser (who are currently on scholarship at the Olympic Training Center) are starting to accumulate such titles as US Senior National Champion, US Open Champion, and Pacific Rim Champion, Swedish Open Champion, and British Open Champion.

Vince Tamura has come a long way since his "first up, first down" days in Fife, Washington. Years of training and love of his art has produced numerous championship titles, a plethora of students who are national and international champions, the legacy of one of the toughest tournaments in the USA, and the revitalization of a jujutsu style.

Bibliography

Svinth, J. (1999). Masato Tamura, Ryoichi Iwakiri, & the Fife Judo Dojo, 1923–1942. *Journal of Asian Martial Arts*, 8(1): 30–43.
Tamura, V. Personal interviews.
Tamura, Y. Personal interviews.
Turnbull, S. (1977). *The samurai: A military history*. Oxford, England: Osprey.
Yoshikawa, E. (1956). *The Heike story*. Boston: Charles E. Tuttle.

Judo & Character: Moving from the Hard to the Gentle Way

by James Behrendt

James Behrendt and the throw that won the
Iowa Amateur Athletic Union Grandchampionship in 1968.

My philosophy of judo was learned the hard way. When I obtained my black belt in 1957, I was caught up in hard training and competition which became the center of my walk in the way. I was extremely fit and strong and I used those natural gifts to eventually defeat the purpose of the judo art. I had discipline but was lacking in spirituality and character. At that time I thought I would excel at the top if I were stronger and quicker than my opponents. I had aspirations of becoming a national or Olympic champion. I almost made it to the Olympics by winning the Iowa State Championships then the regional finals of the Pan Am Games. Those two wins qualified me to train with the Olympic candidates. An injury prevented me from finishing the training.

I won my berth at the nationals four times but never won at that level of competition; in fact the closest I came was placing fourth in Asbury Park, New Jersey. I missed the weight by 4 pounds and had to fight judo players 20 pounds heavier and stronger—players such as Iguchi Motohiko of Japan. Iguchi won the nationals in the heavyweight division. I prolonged my match with him almost to overtime and I thank God he finished me with only a wrenched knee.

Left: James Behrendt in his judo school, October 1968. Right: Young students learning to leg sweep. The younger of the two is James Behrendt's son, Danny. Today, Danny is six feet tall, 200 pounds, and difficult to sweep!

I won dozens of local tournaments over a six-year period and that was not a good thing. I was unbeaten because my competition was weak and I loved the glory of the win. I was actually notorious everywhere in the country for being dangerous on the mat. My first devastating loss in years was when I drew a judo player named Leroy Abe. Abe looked like a slow, plodding, over weight, and out of shape Japanese. The match was in the later rounds and we munched and struggled with each other. With about thirty seconds left before the end of the match, I reminded myself that my strongest technique was on the floor. In desperation, I pulled Leroy upon me with brute strength, thinking that I would turn him over and pin him for thirty seconds for the winning point I thought I deserved. My teammates were aghast because they could only see a hand here and a foot there. It was like being crushed to death; never was I pinned so hard and defeated so badly. I wanted to perform harikiri after the match. I wouldn't have batted an eye if he had won by a decision or a throw, but to lose on the mat was like death. To lose that way was worse than death.

Some of the depression I was experiencing left at the restaurant at the Holiday Inn where we all were staying. I gasped as Leroy walked in with his team. I knew why I had lost. The man looked like a gorilla that had just come off the vine. He was huge; he had large biceps and wrists as big as most ankles; shoulders like coconuts and no neck. The man looked like a power lifter, not a judo player.

I learned my lesson well that day. Another match I lost on a decision was to a brown belt. For me, this was shocking. This brown belt attacked non-stop until time ran out. Being a black belt, I felt I would just defend and after four minutes, pull him to the mat and hold him for the win. The judge tossed the beanbag in and I was stunned. The bag was tossed three minutes into the match because brown belts, at that time, only fought three-minute rounds while black belts fought for five minutes.

That match was in Omaha, Nebraska, five hundred miles from my home in Illinois. Driving home on interstate 80, my car gave out. I asked my wife Marge and our four kids to get out of the car. As they stood by with their mouths wide open, I proceeded to push the four-year-old Mercury station wagon over the cliff. The car went through a barbed wire fence and made a "*the the the*" sound as it passed through the tall row of corn disappearing forever. A half hour later, my best friend and judo student came along and picked us up and drove us to the Greyhound station in Des Moines, Iowa, where we took the bus to Illinois. The kids loved the bus ride back. Poor Marge starred out the window in an almost catatonic stare into vast prairie and corn.

Pushing the car over the cliff exemplified the serious cracks in my character that I mentioned earlier: the strongest was hubris, the sickness of pride. Most religions of the world teach that pride is the deadliest of all sins, because when a person has hubris he is not teachable and never grows spiritually. He just keeps repeating his mistakes over and over without proper reflection or examination of conscience.

In 1992, my 16-year-old son Jimmy was training in a professional boxing stable with Orlin Norris and Jesus Salued, both world champions. Jimmy's coach, Jesse Valdez, had won a silver medal in the Olympics and was a champion in the professional ranks. He told me that young Jimmy had the tools to go all the way to the top in the boxing world because Jimmy out-trained everyone and could hit. Jimmy displayed knock-out power in both hands—a rare gift for a boxer.

Jimmy had another gift: common sense. One day he came home from training and said, "Dad, I'm in a very unique sport because the better I get, the more beat up I get." He made an evaluation: better skills, better opponents and a great chance of permanent brain damage. So he quit, joined a muscle grunt and groan gym, and went for a law degree. The kid is happy he never made it to the top and now boxes for fun, not for wins.

The point I'm making is, be humble enough to know your limitations and be able to accept your fate. Not everybody is a natural judo player. I have taught thousands of young men and women over the past 25 years and found only a small handful of people who had the tools go all the way. I knew of a girl here who was the world champion and when she weighed in she missed the weight by one more pound than I did at Asbury Park, and she was a lightweight. Figure that one out.

When I first came to California in 1969, I worked out in all the strong clubs in Los Angeles and was amazed by one very soft spoken judo player named Tosh Seino. He was a tall lightweight who was the national U.S. champion. An article in a judo magazine written by Kotani Sumiyuki from the Kodokan commented on Tosh. He was commenting on a big event in Chicago, where the All-Japan champions were here bouncing us all over the mats at will. Mentioning Tosh Seino, the commentator said to Kotani that "Tosh is not physically strong. He is just average, not really fast, and his technique is good but not great. How come this man beats everyone he competes against?" Without hesitating, Kotani quickly responded that "*Stukeko* [timing]. The man has perfect timing. The man is gifted, period, and was actually born that way with perfect timing."

That gift must be complimented with humility and peace of emotions. To have perfect timing during attack, and especially defense, one must be free of negative emotions and not be over anxious. If you are over anxious, your reflexes will be exaggerated and slower, although strong. There is definitely something to the samurai who empties his mind when he pulls the sword and becomes the technique. If you have fear, you will tire quickly and be too defensive and eventually make a serious error. If you have anger, you will also tire quickly and be too slow and inaccurate and become a casualty.

James Behrendt teaching some
groundwork with youngsters at his
Rock Island Judo Training Center (1967).

I believe winning judo contests with strength and a strong will to win is not enough. In judo, one must be patient and persistent with humility. When a judo player takes on a new technique and tries to make it part of his offense in a match, it is not always successful at first due to the lack of maturity in that throw or counter. If a judo player is unsuccessful in that technique and loses because of failure to execute it due to the lack of character, the judo player tends to revert back to what worked before. He then chalks up that loss as a learning experience when all that he could learn is that he is pig-headed and not growing into a wholesome person.

I was blessed to have good instruction in judo. I just fell short in learning the virtues needed to be that great champion I lusted to be. In 1956, I was a young marine stationed in Opama, Japan. The Marines paid two Japanese instructors to come on the base to teach judo three times a week for a year. I never missed a class during that year. Instructor Ichinoe Maseo had love coming out of his ears and I eventually befriended him. Ichinoe loved mat work and we would sometimes grapple for two hours straight while the other instructor, Corporal Dame, worked on standing techniques.

Years later he came to visit me in Chicago. Ichinoe was about five foot six and 240 pounds and had huge wide feet that were impossible to move with any type of sweep. His technique was the spring hip throw (*hane goshi*) and when he came to Chicago he lined up twenty black belts and threw them at will with only the spring hip throw. I was spellbound and couldn't believe he could pull that off at fifty plus years of age.

My judo philosophy tells me, if we want to grow and someday resemble judo in a style or the great master Mifune Kyuzo, one must remove personal faults and replace them with virtues. If we were to uncover Mifune's spiritual walk, one would find a wealth of information that would enhance one spiritually and psychologically. Recently, I was watching a televised segment on Japanese Olympic champions. They asked a young man what his favorite part of judo was and he replied: "The hot baths and the fellowship." That was part of his judo. A judo player is more than just a machine. He is a wonderful balanced person. Yamashita of Japan, the greatest judo player of all time, said the same thing. His favorite thing in training was eating with the children and telling them jokes and stories. I experienced a similar thing at a big religious prayer meeting. The priest stated at the coffee and doughnut break that the fellowship at the break was just as important as what goes on in the prayer circle. In summation, character does count, big time. We are not the center of the universe. That spot is reserved for a greater being, however you wish to name it.

As you know, most judo throws are based on circles and you want to be in the center because that is where the power is. Move closer to the center because, in addition to power, peace is there too. Ride on the shirt tails of a power greater than yourself and you will have a Gentle Way.

index

Aizawa, Yasushi, 11
bare-knuckle boxing, 3, 9
Blackwell, Edward, 5
Bregman, Jim, 70, 77
Burns, Martin "Farmer", 6
Butokukai, 50, 66 note 1
Camp Harmony (Puyallup, WA), 73
catch-as-catch-can, 6–7, 20–21, 24
Chicago Yudanshakai (black belt association), 75
Chicago's Jiu-Jitsu Institute, 44, 46–47
Civil War, 20, 29
Colgan, Jim, 75–76
Cornish-style wrestling, 20
criteria of Western sports advocates, 9–10
Cumberland-style wrestling, 20
Devonshire-style wrestling, 20
Draeger, Donn, 10, 75
English small-sword, 2, 5
Fife Dojo, 34–49
Fukuda, Hachinosuke, 75
Fukuda, Keiko, 75
Geesink, Anton, 75
Gotch, Frank, 20–21
gouging, 5–6, 13
Hackenschmidt, Georg, 17, 20–21
Harris, George, 70, 77
Heike-ryu Jujutsu, 70–72
Iizuka, Kunisaburo, 54
Ito, Tokugoro, 25, 27–28
Iwakiri, Ryoichi, 34–39, 41–45, 72
Japanese immigrant (issei), 34, 62
Japanese Ministry of Education, 24
Jiu-Jitsu Institute of America, 46
Kano, Jigoro, 9–11, 19–20, 22–23, 26, 38–39, 41–43, 45, 51, 58, 61, 72, 75
Kato Hiroshi, 56–57, 60, 62
Kaufman, Bill, 74, 76
Kimura, Mitsuo "Mits", 42, 75
Kodokan, 19, 22–23, 42, 50, 54–55, 63–65, 66 note 1, 72, 75, 84,
Koiwai, Eichi (Ei'ichi), 42–43, 53, 58, 61, 65
Kumagai, Yasuyuki, 42–43, 51, 58, 60–61, 72
Kuniyuki, Kaname "Ken", 40, 52, 54, 57–59, 63, 65
Kurosaka Dojo, 50–53

Kurosaka, Hiroshi, 50, 52
manly arts, 2–9, 13
Maruyama, Paul, 70
Mifune, Kyuzo, 75, 86
Minidoka Relocation Center, 44, 64
modern sport, 3–4, 7–12, 14 note 6
muscular Christians, 3, 8
Nadi, Aldo, 7
Nagao, Hic, 74, 76
Nagaoka Hidekazu, 50
Nakat Packing Corporation, 58
Nanka Kodokan Judo Yudanshakai, 65
Nippon Kan Theater, 52–57, 59–62
nisei, 41, 43, 48 note 6, 50, 53–55, 58, 60, 62, 64, 67 note 34, 68 note 47
Nitta, Susumu, 54–58, 62, 65
Okamura, Henry, 74, 76
Osako, John, 74, 76
Pojello, Karl, 73–74
race factor, 8, 14 note 9, 24–25, 27–28, 35
Roosevelt, Theodore, 6, 13 note 3, 26, 29
rough and tumble, 4, 6
Russo-Japanese War, 18
Sakata, Chuji, 51, 56–58, 60–62, 67 note 34
Seattle Dojo, 35–36, 40, 50–53, 55–65, 66 note 14
Seinan Judo Dojo, 59
social class, 3–6, 8–10, 14 note 9
stereotypes, 18, 28
stick, 4–78, 62, 65
Tacoma-Fife Dojo, 45, 47
Taira Clan, 71
Tamura, Hikaru, 35, 39, 42–43, 47
Tamura, Hiroshi, 38, 41, 43–44, 47
Tamura, Masato, 34–46, 56, 58, 62, 76
Tamura, Vince, 46–47, 70–81
Tenshin Shinyo-ryu, 75
Tentoku Kan, 40, 50, 53–65, 66 note 12
Tokyo Metropolitan Police Bureau, 23
Treaty of Amity and Commerce, 22–23
Uemachi Dojo, 59
Westmorland-style wrestling, 20
White River Dojo, 53, 55, 61
World War II, 1–3, 44, 73
wrestling, 3–4, 6–8, 17–21, 24–26, 30, 40–42, 50, 56, 59
Yoshida, Jim, 57–58, 60–65

www.ingramcontent.com/pod-product-compliance
Lightning Source LLC
Chambersburg PA
CBHW070119110526
44587CB00015BA/2490